FOR THE LOVE
of FLIGHT

FOR THE LOVE
of FLIGHT

MARC R. WILLIAMS

To order additional copies of this book, contact:
Xlibris Corporation
1-888-795-4274
www.Xlibris.com
Orders@Xlibris.com
38731

Contents

For my wife Linda Sue,
who made the sacrifices
of a pilot's wife and supported
me during all my crisis.

PROLOGUE

Rarely does anyone think of their emotional and learning disabilities as being assets, beneficial, or that they can even be advantageous.

The book, *For the Love of Flight*, examines the life of a young man who was raised in a struggling family that moved from town to town. This young man attended thirteen different schools before graduating from high school. (Fifteen schools including college.) Because he was enrolled in school at the age of four, he was always one to two years younger than his peers were. So during his school years, he was smaller, less mature than his classmates, and constantly the new kid in school. This made him the target of the school bullies. Add to his emotional baggage dyslexia, ADD (attention deficient disorder), and the subsequent bad grades; it's no wonder that from an early age, he was cast by society to be a failure.

But he had a dream; he wanted to fly. Little did he know that flying would be the therapy, the antidote for the baggage that he was issued and that his ADD made him a natural pilot. But the greatest challenge that he would ever face wouldn't be the missions he flew in Vietnam or the near-fatal flights as a civilian, but his past when it comes back to haunt him. Now as an EMS (Emergency Medical Service) helicopter pilot, he must reach down deep inside himself to once again find his love of flight.

While all of the people are real and events factual, some of the names and the sequence of events have been changed to protect the innocent and their families. You'll understand why later.

CHAPTER 1

The Meltdown

"Where's Lyndon?" I asked, as the paramedic, the flight nurse, and I scurried down the four flights of stairs that lead from the maternity ward, where our ready room is located, down to the helipad.

"It's just on the other side of Osage, just head east," said Paul, our paramedic.

I was grateful that he was born and raised in this area and knew every little town in eastern Kansas like it was his backyard.

At the helipad, where our Bell 206L-3 Emergency Medical Service (EMS) helicopter awaited us, each of us had a duty. Paul unplugged the long extension cord that charged the medical gear. Katie, our petite flight nurse, slid her helmet on and took her position at the nose of the helicopter, ready to pull the battery cart plug as soon as I signaled her. I climbed into the pilot's seat and began my accelerated checklist: rotor brake, off; boost pumps, on; master switch, on; tie-down, removed; caution lights, all working; fuel, on;

stopwatch, on; and throttle, rolled on, then off, past the idle detent. I glanced up at the tip of the main rotor blade once more to make sure that the tie-down was removed and then yelled, "Clear?"

Katie nodded and responded, "Clear." I pressed the Starter button. Although I've started turbine engines thousands of times before, it's still a thrill to hear the sound of the turbine compressor blades winding up, the fuel injectors pumping fuel into the combustion chamber, and the igniters *click-click-clicking* until the fuel ignites with a *chuuuuu*. Now my focus was on the turbine outlet temperature (TOT) gauge. I couldn't add too much fuel, or we'd get a hot start. That would cost the company $100,000 and me, my job. The N1 was now at 58 percent. I released the starter and slowly rolled on the throttle until the detent clicked twice. I turned the generator on and nodded at Katie, her signal to unplug and move the battery cart. I asked over the intercom if they could hear me OK. Both were now in their seats behind me and responded, "Yeah, you're loud and clear."

I felt the vibrator on the pager that was clipped to the left pocket of my dark blue fire-resistant flight suit. OK, I thought, that's dispatch with the Global Positioning System (GPS) coordinates for the scene.

While rolling the throttle up to full RPM, I asked Paul, "Did you get those coordinates?" For backup purposes, all three of us had identical pagers.

"Yeah, let me know when you're ready," he said, knowing that I had my hands full and couldn't enter them into the GPS until we were in the air.

I stopped and took a deep breath. My thoughts went to a core concern. How would the stress of this flight affect me? This was my first scene flight since I was hired, and it was only a month previously that I'd been approved by the FAA to get my second-class flight physical. I lost it a little over a year ago because of post-traumatic stress disorder (PTSD), which, according to the VA, was caused by my experiences in Vietnam. Would I snap? Would I have flashbacks of Vietnam? Or would I experience an anxiety attack? Would my PTSD trigger my obsessive-compulsive disorders (OCD)? Every little thing would cause me to remember randomly any of the myriads of mistakes that I've made in life, even as far back as when I was five years old. With each memory retrieved, I would respond with an involuntary "damn!" either silently or all too often auditable. Yeah, I know, I've got baggage, but at least I didn't have to worry about my attention deficit disorder (ADD). My ADD actually helps me while flying. Strange at it may sound, but what everybody considers a disability is actually an asset to me, at least when I'm flying. And my dyslexia is more of an irritant than a concern. Like when I glance at a restroom's Women sign, I see Men and walk in. So I've learned to look at words closely and then for evidence of a urinal.

"Oh brother, what am I doing here?" I whispered to myself. Then, "Coming up," I calmly called out over the intercom, hiding any evidence of my internal struggle.

Paul and Katie glanced out their windows to make sure that no one was approaching the helicopter or, more likely, that I forgot to remove the ladder that I used for the preflight of the aircraft.

"You're clear right . . . clear left."

Raising the collective and adding just enough left pedal to keep us straight, I brought us up to a three-foot hover. The torque gauge read 88 percent. That was good. We wanted no more than 90 percent in order to get out of the Newman Hospital helicopter pad, surrounded by buildings, trees, and streetlights. We call it "the hole." Without stopping at a three-foot hover, I continued to pull the collective until the torque gauge read 100 percent. Now we were going straight up. At about one hundred feet, enough to clear all the obstacles, I pushed forward on the cyclic (the control stick between my knees), making the nose pitch down just a little bit, but enough to start us moving forward. The bird shuddered like a child taking its first taste of a lemon. That was translational lift. It meant that the air had changed its direction and was now going through the rotor blades from the front. I lowered the collective to 80 percent, and we took up an easterly heading while cruising over the houses and waving children, just three hundred feet over their heads.

"OK, Paul, what do you have?" I asked while getting the GPS ready to program with my left hand.

"Three eight three eight by nine five three three, we're going to a farmhouse about two and a half miles northeast of Lyndon; they're setting up an LZ in his backyard."

By "LZ," he meant landing zone. I repeated the coordinates as I entered them into the GPS, taking turns between looking at the GPS at the bottom of the instrument panel and looking outside the helicopter.

Now I called Life Team dispatch on the FM radio. "Dispatch, Life Team 21's off base at 32, 480 pounds of fuel, three souls on board, and an ETE (estimated time en route) of eighteen minutes."

While Life Team dispatch read back my report, I could hear Katie contacting Osage County EMS to get a status on the fifty-five-year-old male who appeared to be having a heart attack. After they gave Katie his vitals, I heard them estimate that the patient weighed about 220 pounds.

I did the math in my head that we'd burn about seventy-five pounds of fuel flying to the scene. And with a 220-pound patient, we should end up about thirty pounds under gross weight leaving the scene.

Katie repeated the patient's condition and then asked for the LZ info.

"Marc, did you get the patient's weight at 220 pounds?" she quickly asked, while waiting for the fireman who was responsible for the LZ to come back with the LZ's description.

"Yeah, we're going to be fine," I responded, knowing that my crew needed to feel assured that we'd be able to get out of this poor guy's backyard.

Feel assured? Hell, I'm not even sure of myself, I thought. I went right back to that series of what-ifs that plagued me just before liftoff. Did I make a mistake taking this job? Sure, I love to fly, but flying EMS is no Sunday afternoon joyride. Can I take the pressure? I now felt a wave of goose bumps envelope my whole body. Aw crap, is this the beginning of an anxiety attack?

"Come on, Marc," I said under my breath, "you're still good, and you still have what it takes. Your whole life has been about flying." Flying requires confidence, and flying EMS requires a lot of it; and right now, mine was quickly draining out like water out of a bathtub. I needed to get my head screwed on straight; I needed self-confidence, and I need it now. It had to come from within. I took a deep breath and allowed my mind to reminisce. To think back to how I got here. "OK, Marc, remember who you are! Remember, how flying has effected your whole life and remember what you have had to overcome for the love of flight."

CHAPTER 2

The Search Begins

It actually wasn't that far from here where my love for flight began. I was born in Marysville, Kansas, into a long line of dry land farmers. That's another way of saying that we were dirt-poor. But my emotional baggage that I grew accustomed to carrying didn't come from our being poor, nor is it related to my being from a small all-white town in Kansas. Yeah, besides the PTSD and ADD, I had other problems. I was just a normal kid with two annoying brothers who were both older than I was. My mom, Ella Mae, came from a family that owned the largest turkey farm in the state of Kansas. It was about five miles west of Marysville. She was lucky enough to be raised with more comforts than the average farmer's daughter. However, my dad, Royal, wasn't as fortunate. He was the oldest of four, two boys and two girls, and was eight years old when his dad died from Rocky Mountain spotted fever. So from an early age, he had to be the man of the house and run the small family farm. Although he could have had a draft deferment because of being a farmer, he joined the army early on during World War II. While in France, he was severely wounded by shrapnel that I assume came from an artillery shell. "You see," he said; that's how he started all of his conversations, "I was sitting on my helmet playing poker when a bomb blew up behind me."

That's all he'd say. I never did find out if it was true or not, but knowing him, it probably was. My dad's younger brother, Uncle Trarze, told me on the day of Dad's funeral, which was about ten years ago, that Dad was a paraplegic for a time after being wounded. He said it was because of the shrapnel that was lodged next to his spinal column. Dad suffered back pain for the rest of his life because of that shrapnel, but he did receive some disability payment from the government. About every night, before going to bed, he'd drink two glasses of brandy. He wasn't mean when he drank. In fact, he was quite talkative. He picked me out from my two brothers to share his ideas on how he was going to get rich. Looking back, I guess that I was probably the only one, in or outside of the family, that would take him seriously; and it allowed me to stay up late. Alcoholic? Yeah, he probably was, but that's how his generation, who fought a terrible war, self-medicated. There weren't any fancy neurological drugs back then, and PTSD hadn't been discovered yet. Many men, like my dad, drank to ease their physical and mental pain. Yeah, they were a whole generation of alcoholics.

Back then, farm boys knew only one thing and that was farming. And since Dad couldn't farm anymore, he tried the railroad but was fired. Then he became a salesman, and a lousy one at that. But he tried.

Mom went to work at the local drugstore to help supplement our income; and since my grandmother, the turkey raiser, didn't want to take care of me, Mom enrolled me in kindergarten at the age of four. Now here's where I started to be issued my first dose of emotional baggage.

My parents, brothers and me with my favorite airplane

The psychologist, I. P. Christensen, wrote: Physically, adolescence is marked by the development of sexual maturity. The adolescent becomes unable to ignore other-sex peers and begins to feel sexual and romantic attraction to them. Early-maturing boys have considerable social advantages. They are more popular with their fellows, girls, and adults than are late maturers, who are rated as less attractive, childish, bossy, and dependent.

That fits me to a tee! Not only was I a late bloomer, I was at least a year to a year-and-a-half younger than my classmates were. It gets worse.

Now, here's my second dose of baggage. By the midfifties, my dad was trying to sell life insurance to dirt-poor farmers, and it just wasn't working. I don't know how, but he heard of work in Idaho; so he borrowed some money and moved us all to Nampa. Actually, I think he just wanted to get away from his in-laws who never did like him. So off to Nampa we went. Well, the job didn't pan out. We ended up delivering newspapers in the morning, evening, and then during the day; like a family of migrant workers, we hoed sugar beets. I really didn't mind so much, but I could tell that my dad had hit bottom. We got word that my dad's mom, my grandmother, died. And it was just a couple of weeks later that Dad lost his disability pension. He said the IRS got it.

Since Idaho didn't work out, Dad borrowed some more money; and we moved to Albuquerque, New Mexico. He started selling cemetery lots, and with a measure of success. But this didn't last long. He said his boss wouldn't give him all the commissions that were due him. So off we went, this time to Denver, Colorado. But it was the same old song, "Beat me out of my money!" We moved to Manhattan, Kansas, and then on to Las Cruces, New Mexico.

It was about this time that puberty hit me pretty hard, and I was growing at what seemed like an inch a week. I was a junior at Las Cruces High School; and not only was I the new kid and poor, but my pants were all too short, "high waters." The kids would laugh and point at my pants' bottoms ending right above my ankle. On the outside, I'd act unconcerned and reply, "In Manhattan, where I just moved from, high waters were the style." I didn't tell them that it was Manhattan, Kansas, and not Manhattan, New York. They actually seemed to believe me.

It was here that I met Paula, a rich girl, who, for some reason, fell for me. She was a beautiful young girl who entered beauty contests and went to charm school. And like everyone else in my class, she was a year older than I was and more mature. Did I say she was rich? She actually had her own car, a new Mercury Comet! My parents really liked her, probably because her family had money, but more likely it was because they treated my parents with respect, something my dad got very little of.

Paula and I were really enjoying our new relationship when Dad dropped the bomb.

"We gotta move; they beat me out of my money."

This was not good. Oh, I hated everything about Las Cruces, but I was firmly infatuated with Paula. Paula was a trooper and understood that I had to go, but I could tell that this was crushing her, which made me feel even worse. No amount of arguing with Dad helped my cause. It just made him feel bad.

Now it was off to Hobbs, New Mexico, for another cemetery sales job. I really felt sorry for my mom and dad. And for the first time, I felt sorry for me. I'd attended twelve schools since Mom enrolled me in kindergarten, and now I was about to start the "new kid" process all over again in school number 13.

Yeah, I had all the typical problems of a late bloomer, plus I was always the new kid in school – smaller, more immature, and thus the prime target of the class bully. Some say that this will make a kid tougher, like naming your son Sue as in the Johnny Cash song. Well, maybe that's true for some kids, but it didn't work for me. Not only that I wasn't tougher, I didn't like to fight and didn't want to fight. I just wanted to be friends with everyone. There were times when I should have knocked the crap out of other boys, but I didn't. Some would say that I was a bigger man (or boy) for not fighting. That it took more courage not to fight than to fight. I'd like to say it was based on some higher principle, but I was actually afraid; and I felt like a coward. I know everybody wants to be liked, but I had some real issues. And so to my laundry list of screwed up baggage, you can add insecurity.

CHAPTER 3

The Love of Flight

Perhaps my insecurity explained why, while growing up, I didn't need anyone to play with. Alone with my imagination, I would play for hours by myself. I was a daydreamer, and my grades reflected it. Every day, my teachers would interrupt the imagined flight of my rocket ship (my pencil) and bring me back to Earth to a subject that I didn't understand nor cared for. What I was interested in was anything that had to do with flight. At home, two chairs pushed together, facing each other, was my cockpit; and an old football helmet was my pilot's helmet. At the age of four, I got in trouble with my mother for tearing out all of the airplane pictures from the "A" volume of our family encyclopedia and hiding them under the bookcase. My dad didn't seem to mind. He knew I just wanted to fly.

Something wonderful happened while we lived in Nampa, Idaho. On my eighth birthday, my parents took me out to eat at the restaurant of my choice. I chose the restaurant that was inside the passenger terminal building at the Boise Airport! I was in heaven, watching airplanes come and go while eating shrimp. My brothers didn't go along; Mom and Dad couldn't afford to take the whole family out to eat. And come to think of it; they didn't order anything but coffee.

After lunch, they took me next door to a flight school. A chance to get up close to a real airplane and a pilot too! I was thrilled to say the least. The sign on the side of the hangar read Airplane Rides $5.

We stopped short of the door, and Dad asked, "You wanna go up, son?"

"WOW! Do I!" I replied with a big grin on my face.

My first airplane ride! This is it, I thought, a chance to taste my dream. I'd always dreamed of flight. Although I don't remember it, my mom's brother, Uncle Bill, told me that when we lived in Marysville, I told him that I had a dream in which I was in an airplane that was spinning toward the ground.

He asked me, "How did you get out of that?"

"I hit myself on the side of my head and woke myself up."

But now this was real – no more imaginary airplanes. I was going to fly in a real one.

As we walked in the door, I noticed that the office was cluttered with aircraft parts, cans of oil, and aviation magazines. I could smell the space heater that was pumping out more heat than was necessary over by the window that faced the empty ramp. I thought to myself, Where is everybody? This place should be full of people who want to fly. Maybe the pilot was up flying with a student, or maybe his airplane was broke. Anyway, I knew this was too good to be true. Just then, a man opened the door that led into the hangar and walked into the office. As he wiped his hands with a rag, he asked, "Can I help you?"

My dad responded, "This is my son's eighth birthday, and he'd like an airplane ride."

The pilot now turned his attention to me and asked, "Ever been flying before, son?"

The pilot was just what I expected, a good-looking tall man with a square chin and a pilot's mustache. Oops, there goes my imagination again. Actually, he was just an average-looking guy with the beginnings of a potbelly, a receding hairline, and no mustache. But to me, he was my hero – a real pilot. I'd never met a pilot before. He was special in my mind, with his swagger of confidence, not arrogance. He had something special that very few people had – the ability to fly. But today, he didn't mind sharing it with an eight-year-old boy on this birthday. Everybody's got to like him, I thought. After all, he can fly.

"No, sir, I've never been flying," I responded, but I wanted to say more about my dream – how I practiced flying in my imaginary airplane and . . . but I didn't.

As he started to turn toward the hangar door, he said, "Well, let's go see what we can find to fly."

The aircraft of his choice was sitting at the front of the opened hangar. It was a two-seat (front and back) fabric-covered "tail dragger" called a Culver Cadet. He pushed the grey-colored aircraft out of the hangar to the ramp and said to me, "Why don't you get up front?"

I thought, Of course, I want to sit up front; that's where the pilot sits, isn't it? But I replied, "Yes, sir."

He put me in the front seat and buckled me in then climbed into the backseat. There in front of me was a stick, or it looked more like a hollow rod with a handle on it. Although I couldn't reach them, I could see two pedals that must be where the feet go.

I wondered if I should be holding the stick. After all, from watching flying movies, I knew that that's how you fly the airplane. They all started moving back and forth and then stopped. He opened the side window, yelled "clear!", and then hit the starter. The small engine came to life. Oh man, this is scary, I thought, but I can't chicken out now; this is what I've always dreamed about. The engine was louder than I thought it would be. We immediately started to move forward. We made a right turn on another taxiway and continued to taxi out to the runway but stopped short. The man revved up the engine but didn't go anywhere. I didn't know why, but I trusted him. He pulled the power back some and then taxied on to the runway. He pointed the airplane down the runway. I couldn't see ahead of us; I was too short to see over the instrument panel, and this disappointed me. The disappointment quickly left when he put the throttle full forward.

Wow! Here we go!

The tail quickly came off the ground, and ever so smoothly, we lifted in the air. I could see plenty now. My first airplane ride! Everything on the ground looked so small, like toys. The old-timer (everybody over twenty-one was an old-timer to me) told me about dropping off Santa at a store below us. Not sure how he did that but I believed him. We stayed in the air for about fifteen minutes, but that was the best fifteen minutes of my short life. Then it was time to come in for a landing. Everything on the ground was getting bigger and bigger until we leveled off just above the runway, and suddenly, we were on the ground. WOW, I said to myself. That was a smooth landing! I hadn't even felt the wheels touch the runway. Oops, I spoke too soon – *ker plop*! Yeah, I felt that landing. We taxied up in front of the hangar where my parents were proudly waiting for their little boy. I sure loved them for making this sacrifice for me. As I got out of the airplane, I had an eight-year-old's grin on my face. I couldn't stop talking about every second of that life-changing fifteen minutes.

The pilot, who was also the flight school owner, got such a kick out of my enthusiasm for flight that he didn't even charge my dad the $5 for the ride. (Thinking back, I believe he was probably just embarrassed because of the landing.) To this day, whenever I take kids up for their first airplane or helicopter ride, I think back on that flight and tell their parents, "This one's on me."

CHAPTER 4

Lesson One

I was sixteen when we moved to Hobbs, New Mexico. I completed the last semester of my junior year and all of my senior year at Hobbs High School. I couldn't believe it. It seemed like I spent my entire life going to school; and now at the old age of seventeen, I was about to graduate. For their graduation present, other kids were getting new cars or paid tuition for college or trade school. Me? My dad gave me a $100 bill. Back in '67, that was a lot of money, at least for our family. I realized that it meant a bill didn't get paid that month.

As he handed me my graduation present, he said, "Son, why don't you take the $100 and give it to Dale Johnson, who owns Seminole Flying Service, and learn to fly?"

WOW! Great idea, Dad!

I guess Dad sold Dale some cemetery property and set this all up with him. So the following Saturday morning, I took that $100 bill, borrowed my brother's car, and drove to Seminole, Texas, which is about thirty miles east of Hobbs. This was to be the down payment on my flying career. Man! This was exciting. I was actually going to learn to fly!

The airport, which was located about five miles west of Seminole, was a small country airport with a few private aircraft hangars and Dale's two larger hangars where he kept his two crop dusters. On the north side of those hangars was a small office and bathroom.

When I walked into the office, I felt the feeling like I've been there before. Then it occurred to me. This was just like the office of the flight school in Boise where I got my first airplane ride. Aircraft parts were lying around, and aviation magazines scattered on the coffee table in front of an old sofa fresh out of the Goodwill Store. And the smell. A combination of dust, motor oil, and the space heater that was putting out more heat than was necessary.

Dale looked up from a six-inch stack of papers that covered the small desk at the not-so-far end of the combination office/pilot lounge.

"Can I help you?"

"Hi, I'm Marc Williams, and my dad said I should come by and give you this; and you'd teach me to fly."

Dale stood up and walked over to me and held his hand out. "Well, it's nice to meet you, Marc."

Dale was wearing matching khaki pants and shirt and a big smile. Just what I'd expect from a real pilot. He appeared to be in his mid to late thirties, clean-shaven, and about six-foot-two-inches tall. Dale was a good-looking man with sandy hair. I already liked him, maybe because he was nice to me but more likely it was because he had that same swagger as the man who gave me my first airplane ride had. Dale was a pilot, a crop duster, and my hero.

Dale just bought an old 1946 Cessna 140, and he was going to use it to teach all of his students to fly. I guess I was going to be his first student. We walked out of the office and into the hangar where this proud bird sat. I was sure that she was waiting for me. This had to be the most beautiful airplane in the world. It was a high-wing tail dragger with two seats, side by side. The radio didn't work, the right brake would fade, and the light blue trim that accented the polished aluminum skin (that wasn't so polished) was faded and chipped. Oh, she was a beauty. And since I was Dale's only student, I felt like she was all mine! I called her *Jenny*. That was the name of my favorite airplane, a World War I biwing training airplane. Now my favorite airplane was a faded blue, unpolished 1946 Cessna 140.

Regarding the brakes, Dale preached, "Ya', don't need 'em; they're only for parking anyway." I believed every word that came out of his mouth. I must have had that same silly eight-year-old's grin on my face because after my first lesson, Dale hired me as his flag boy.

Since there wasn't a lot of money floating around at our house, I learned early on that if I wanted something, I'd have to come up with the money myself. That meant going out and getting a job. So at the age of fourteen, I started selling fruits at a roadside market then

"The Taxmen" I'm on the far left

moved on to washing dishes at a hamburger joint. I used my wages to buy a bass guitar and amplifier; and by the time we moved to

Hobbs, I could play it pretty good. Except that I kept losing my focus, resulting in losing my place during a song. Oh well, we played so loud that, that probably didn't matter. But since there weren't many kids with a bass and amplifier, it didn't take long for me to get into a band that played dances on Saturday nights. True, $20 a night wasn't bad, but working for Dale, that was the high point of my young career. I actually got to handle airplanes! Well, I washed them anyway. Plus I had a front row seat for my own personal air show.

Without some kind of reference point, it was difficult for a crop duster to know exactly where he had just dusted. So with a red flag in hand, I became that reference point. I would stand at one end of the half-mile-long field, and Dale would line his sights up on me and swoosh. That's when the air show began. Closely following the rows of cotton, the Piper Pawnee would dance just a foot or two above the cotton plants, trailing a white cloud of chemicals. Now came the hard part of my job, counting off thirteen rows, then standing there holding up the red flag. How could a high school graduate keep on losing count? After completing the pass, Dale pulled the Pawnee up into a steep, climbing right turn, and then quickly reversed it to a climbing left turn. And after reversing his direction, he'd push the nose over into a dive aiming the single-seat airplane at the boy with the red flag. The process would go on for most of the day or until the winds picked up and started blowing the chemicals to the neighboring fields, which was a no – no.

After working for Dale for about a month, he sent me to Dalhart, Texas, to help Walt, his part-time spray pilot. Walt was a really nice guy who probably felt sorry for me. No, he really did feel sorry for me. He saw my love for flight but also that I had a difficult time remembering and complying with Dale's instructions. Walt was a professional air-show pilot, which meant that he could do no wrong in my eyes. In the evening after we were through for the day, he would practice his routine over the small Seminole airport. People would pull off the highway just to watch his routine. He was a great pilot. He even took me up in his clipped-wing Taylorcraft, his air-show airplane, and introduced me to aerobatics. WOW! Then, like the rights of adoption into the aviation family, he gave me his old wooden prop. That meant so much to me. Walt was not only a great pilot, he was also a good man. Man, I loved that guy. Unfortunately, I later lost that prop when our belongings were used as collateral for one of my dad's unpaid debts.

I guess it was about the middle of June when Dale sent me and Walt to Dalhart to spray some cotton. He flew one of Dale's Pawnees, and I drove Dale's old beige-colored Ford work truck and pulled the chemical trailer.

That night after we checked into our hotel, he took me to supper and then to a local carnival. He took me under his wing and gave me instructions on how to deal with people. He taught me how to hold myself up and be proud. "After all, Marc, you're a pilot (student)."

I didn't realize it at the time, but he recognized that I had very little self-esteem; and he was trying to build me up.

The next morning, we went out to the Dalhart airport where Walt got the Pawnee ready while I hooked up to the chemical trailer. He drew a map of where we were going to spray that day; and while handing me the piece of paper, he said, "Marc, if you have difficulty finding the field, just look for me; I'll be circling it."

How kind. He took in consideration my limitations and made provisions for me. It worked. Sure enough, I got confused and lost. I stopped alongside the road and climbed up on the bed of the truck.

There he was, about two miles away, circling. Not only did he solve my problem, but he saved what little self-respect that I had left.

By the time I arrived on the scene, Walt had already landed and parked the Pawnee half on the road and half in the ditch. He had me park the trailer far enough off the road so that he could get by it with the airplane.

The plan was that I would attach the chemical trailer's hose to the receptacle on the left side of the aircraft, fill the Pawnee's hopper with chemicals, and then he would take off and spray the field. He said that the fields were small and didn't need for me to mark them. Actually, I think that he didn't want to give me more to do than what I could handle. I guess he figured that filling up the plane's hopper would max me out. He's probably right.

And so, that's how it worked for a good part of the day. Walt would land the Pawnee on the dirt road heading into the wind toward me and the trailer. While the engine was still running, I would fill up the hopper. Once full, he'd taxi down the road in the opposite direction of his landing, turn around in a farmer's front yard, and take off back toward me, into the wind. Heavily loaded with chemicals, he would barely clear me, the pickup, and the chemical trailer. I think he was just trying to scare me. But it didn't work; I loved it!

On the last run of the day, Walt yelled out to me from the small opened window that after filling up his hopper, I was to take the truck and trailer back to the airport where he'd meet me. I gave him the thumbs-up. I can handle that; after all, the whole day went by, and I didn't make a single mistake. So after unplugging the chemical hose from the Pawnee, Walt headed down the road just like the dozen times before; but this time he added full throttle. The engine roared, and the propeller blew dust all over me. I didn't mind. The Pawnee started to slowly roll down the road toward the farmhouse. I thought that I'd wait a minute before I started to head toward the airport. I wanted to watch my friend take off, especially since he was taking off downwind, with a heavy load and on a hot day.

As the Pawnee gained more speed, its tail finally lifted off the road. Now I'm getting concerned. He was coming up on the farmhouse where he'd been turning around, and he's still on the ground. Then all of sudden, as if choreographed perfectly, the farmer's wife pulls her Ford Fairlane out of the farmer's driveway onto the dirt road heading straight at Walt.

"Oh no, they're going to hit!" I yelled, but there was no one around to hear me.

The farmer's wife slammed on the brakes, stopping her car in the middle of the road. At the same time, Walt pulled the Pawnee off the ground, just barely clearing the roof of the car, and then he fell back to the ground. After bouncing two or three times, he pulled the overweight pelican off the ground and started to make a slow right turn toward the unfinished field. The poor lady was frozen; she didn't move. I didn't know if she had a heart attack or what; she just sat there. I wondered if I should go check on her but decided that it's better that she didn't know who was responsible for the near miss. Anyway, she was probably trying to clean up her mess.

We continued spraying cotton for the next two days, and then it was back to Seminole. Neither one of us brought up the close call that occurred on that dirt road in Dalhart. No doubt, Walt learned something from it as did I. I think the lesson I learned was more profound than his: "Even people who you think are perfect make mistakes but that doesn't make them a bad person or a bad pilot. That applies to me too, the king of mistakes, but not that bad of a pilot."

Shortly after we got back, Walt packed his bags and moved on. I guess he went on to fly air shows somewhere. I'll never forget the kind respect he showed me, a tall, lanky kid that had a whole lot of growing up to do.

I loved every day that I worked for Dale. I couldn't think of anything else I'd rather do, except fly. Yep, I wanted to be a crop duster. At the end of the day, when I finished washing his plane, I'd get a flying lesson in my little bird. I never got a paycheck. My wages were the flying lessons, and that was just fine with me. But it was hard on the social life of a seventeen-year-old, so I continued to play dances on the weekends to get spending money. My life was beginning to change. My spare time was normally spent hanging out with the guys in the band, learning new songs, and doing things we ought not. They really weren't a good influence on me, but they seemed to like me; or really, they just needed a bass player. And I was pretty good. Of course, they were older than me, more mature, and so on; and that led to some arguments and near fights. I didn't like that, so more and more of my time was spent just hanging around out at the airport and flying my *Jenny*.

With eight hours of dual flight instruction, I soloed. This consisted of three takeoffs and landings from the crop duster strip. The first two landings were as smooth as glass, but the third one, well, that was about as good as the one on my first ride in Idaho. But hey, that's not too bad. Any pilot who has ever flown a tail dragger would attest to that. Dale wrote in my pilot's logbook, "First Super Solo." I thought that was a nice thing to put in my logbook! Years later, after I became a flight instructor, I realized that he had just abbreviated "supervised." Oh well, to me it was a "super" solo.

For the first time in my life, I started to like myself. A spark of self-esteem! I was good, real good.

After my second supervised solo, Dale didn't pay much attention to me and just let me fly whenever I wanted. After work or on the weekends, I'd just pull *Jenny* out of the hangar and take off. This isn't quite how things are done in the flying world, but West Texas had its own set of rules.

It seemed like the winds always blew in West Texas; and since I didn't know any better, I'd fly anyway. But on one clear, cloudless, and of course, windy day, I was confronted with a problem. This would be the first of the many that I would face during my career as a pilot. I took off like on any other day and flew around for about fifteen minutes, looking at the scenery, and flying down next to the cars and trucks, waving my wings at people. Then I decided to do a couple of touch-and-gos. Well, the wind sock indicated that the wind had picked up, no problem, but the wind direction wasn't down the runway like it has been in the past. Really, it wasn't even close. It was blowing at a forty-five-degree angle off to the side of the runway. This hadn't come up before. And Dale hadn't taught me how to make a crosswind landing. I didn't realize the extent of my problem until I lined up on final approach to the gravel strip; and as I leveled off at about ten feet above the runway, the wind blew me off the runway over the mesquite trees.

I quickly realized that this wasn't healthy, so I added full throttle; and looking like Dale making a pass over the cotton fields, I "dusted" the mesquite trees until I could get enough airspeed to climb out. I tried the same routine again and with the same results. I was thinking that maybe I should land on the shorter and narrower crosswind runway, which was located on the south end of the main runway and lined up at a ninety-degree angle. So I reentered the traffic pattern and lined up on final approach to the other runway.

My, this is a short runway, I thought. But the results were the same, except this time I drifted off to the left side, still over the mesquite trees. For the first time, I felt something that I'd become very familiar with in the future, *dread*. Am I going to crash? Is this the end of my short-lived flying career?

"OK, what should I do?" I asked myself out loud.

I remembered reading in my pilot's training manual about how to make a "wheel landing." This is a landing wherein the two main wheels touch the runway first, keeping the aircraft firmly on the runway; and then as the aircraft slows down, the tail should gently come down until the tail wheel touches the runway. I thought that's what I need to do. But it's an advanced maneuver that experienced tail-dragger pilots find difficult to master, and some never do. But I didn't have a choice.

Here goes, I thought. I lined up on the runway, just like the normal approach that I was used to making. But as I got over the runway, I left a little power in it so that I continued to fly just a little lower and lower until the main wheels touched the runway. I did it! Instinctively, not wanting the aircraft to leave the ground, I pushed forward slightly on the elevator. This put more weight on the main wheels. Then I slowly pulled back on the throttle; and sure enough, just as the manual promised, she slowed down; and the tail wheel gently touched down on the runway. Wow! I had to say, I was very proud of myself. I was a real pilot.

However, this great act of airmanship didn't seem to improve my decision-making abilities. A large and obnoxious high-school classmate of mine, who took pleasure in roughing me up for what he considered fun (I really hated that), wanted me to take him flying, since I was now a hotshot pilot. I knew I shouldn't do it. Dale told me that student pilots were strictly forbidden by the FAA from carrying passengers. Why'd I say yes? Damn peer pressure!

I picked him up on a Sunday afternoon, and we drove the twenty-five minutes from Hobbs to Seminole. Why didn't I make him drive himself? Maybe he would have gotten lost – problem solved. All the while we were heading east to the Seminole Airport, my conscience was killing me. I knew that I shouldn't do this, but I couldn't tell him that I wasn't qualified. He'd tell everybody, wouldn't he? Fortunately, Dale wasn't there, so I pulled the aircraft out of the hanger and did a quick preflight. I wanted to get out of there before anybody showed up. I pried him into the right seat and strapped him in. My goodness, I thought, he must weigh three hundred pounds! Can we even get off the ground with this behemoth? He then put on a stupid-looking World War I aviator's cap. Oh brother! I just wanted to get this over with. I taxied out to the runway, checked the magnetos, and then applied full throttle. I noticed right off that it was taking us longer to gather speed. Then finally, the tail came off the ground. We went faster and faster, but *Jenny* didn't want to fly. Oh, great! We're going to off the end of the runway! I pulled back on the controls (elevator), and she finally gave in and came off the ground. Here I go again, dusting the mesquite trees. As we gained airspeed, we began to gain some altitude. I didn't want to fly him over Seminole in fear that Dale may notice that I was flying and come out to the airport to see how I was doing, which would have been a first. So I made a right turn and flew west of the airport for a couple of minutes and then headed back. It was a miserable five-minute flight, no flying next to the cars and no touch-and-gos. This was one of the few flights that I didn't enjoy. Nothing happened, other than I landed a little hard, no doubt because of lard butt. The FAA didn't show up, and Dale never learned about it. But it didn't matter. I hated myself for doing something so stupid for someone I didn't even like! Lesson learned, I hoped.

Dale taught me a lot about flying, like if you chase cars down the road, don't do it heading into the sun. "With the sun in your eyes," he said, "you might not see the power lines, and they will bring you out of the sky for sure. And when you're on final approach for a landing and you see a station wagon with blue license plates parked in front of the office, do a go-around and don't land until it's gone. That's the FAA."

Dale sure didn't like the FAA. Maybe it was because he had two Piper Pawnee spray planes, both of which had the same N numbers! (Those are the FAA numbers that are on the side of the airplane, the first letter of which is *N*.) I guess he figured he could insure two for the price of one.

Dale became more and more disgruntled with me because of an assortment of blunders that most seventeen-year-olds would make. At least that's what I kept telling myself. I was always getting the chemical trailer stuck, the pickup truck stuck, and the car stuck . . . Hell, I got everything stuck. But the final straw was when he dumped a litter of live kittens into the trash barrel. I guess he didn't want any more cats around, but I just felt that that wasn't right. So I carefully plucked them right back out of the barrel. It wasn't a great career move.

"Marc," Dale said, exasperated, "I think you might wanna go home and think about things for a while." That was the West Texas way for saying, "You're fired!"

CHAPTER 5

Tough Love

Flying was now in my blood. I really didn't want to do anything else but be around airplanes and pilots, and I didn't want to work anywhere else except at an airport. The only other airport in the area that had a flight school was in Hobbs. So after saving the kittens, I went home and got cleaned up and went out to the Lea County Airport. Actually, it seemed like JFK Airport compared to the Seminole Airport. I pulled into the parking lot of Marshall Aviation, opened the all-metal door, and walked into the small lobby that was attached to a large metal hangar. The lobby had a counter, a couple of chairs, a small table

that separated them, a community bathroom, and a small office. This was Dick and Ann's office, which I would become very familiar with. Dick walked out of his office and asked, "Looking for something to fly?"

WOW, how'd he know?

It turned out that this was Dick's way of greeting everyone who walked in the door. Dick was in his early forties and about two inches shorter than me, which would make him about five feet ten inches tall. He was a little overweight and growing bald. He was a very experienced pilot, but his swagger was different from the other pilots. Dick was a businessman first. Although he was a pilot, he didn't seem to love it.

Without mentioning the cat incident, I told Dick that I used to work for Dale Johnson but was looking for a job a little closer to home. He hired me on the spot. (I still had that eight-year-old's grin.) Dick and his wife Ann became my second parents.

Like Dale, Dick too had a lot of advice for me. "Don't get married! Stay out of the army!" And "If the FAA comes in, you talk to 'em, because I won't." Dick too? What was wrong with the FAA? I guessed that dislike for the FAA ran rampant in West Texas and Eastern New Mexico.

Dick had a Piper Aircraft distributorship, flight school, air-taxi operation, and he sold aircraft fuel. My job was to park and fuel transient aircraft and pull aircraft in and out of the large hangar for customers. I wore red coveralls and waved two green flags at aircraft as they taxied in after they landed. I was one motivated young man. I made two cents a gallon for refueling aircraft. I couldn't believe it. I was actually making money for something that I'd do for free, and I was enjoying every minute of it. After parking an aircraft, I'd go up to the door and ask, "Where'd 'ja come in from? How's the flight? Need some fuel?" Was I just being polite? Not me, I really wanted to know and then sell them some fuel. Instead of being the only pilot, like over at Dale's, I was surrounded by pilots; and pilots love to talk to pilots. That's called "hangar talk." And I was soaking it all up. This was great, just like a club.

I'm sorry to say that I didn't run out of mistakes to make while working for Dale. Dick and Ann were very patient with me, like when I overfilled the gas truck and jet fuel ran over the top like a waterfall. I didn't know fuel expanded when it warmed up. Or the times (yeah, that's plural) I left the gas caps and oil caps off a number of aircraft. I even directed a Cessna 150 into a telephone pole while the pilot was watching my directions. Oops! I didn't bother to ask them my normal series of questions. To my surprise, Dick stuck up for me and said that the pilot was responsible for his own aircraft. I think he knew that since I was his employee, he was responsible for my actions; and he didn't want to pay for my mistake. But it was nice of him anyway.

Mickey Monk was now my flight instructor. I really liked Mickey; he was what I thought pilots should be like, and I wanted to be like him. Yes, he had the pilot's swagger. Nothing rattled him, and he took everything in stride. He didn't talk a lot; but when he did, pilots listened. He told me the story that had to be the ultimate cool. When he was about my age, he bought a Cessna 140 like the one Dale had; and he took his new bride on their honeymoon in it. Yeah, he was my hero, but he wasn't his wife's hero. She gave him fits. Maybe that's why he was always at the airport.

As a line boy, I got to know most of the rich and famous people in Hobbs. Since Hobbs was in the middle of nowhere, people who could afford it used private aircraft to get to the big city. I was accustomed to pulling their aircraft out of the hangar, making sure it was fueled, cleaning the windows, and helping them load their baggage. Quite often, I would ask them where they were going, and they'd say "Albuquerque"; but as I watched them climb out after takeoff they'd head southwest, toward El Paso and Juarez, Mexico, I caught on pretty quick.

One Saturday morning, I pulled the Cherokee Six out of the hangar, which was scheduled for a 9:00 a.m. departure. This was a beautiful single-engine, low-wing airplane with six seats, and it could carry anything you could put in it. As was my routine, I made sure that it was full of fuel, cleaned the windshield, and wiped the bug stains off the wings. Four men in their early thirties showed up, one of whom, the pilot, I knew. This was Larry Shed. "Hi, Larry, where ya' going?"

"Albuquerque, to the state fair," he responded as he did his preflight. Rather, it was more like a jog around the aircraft to see if it still had two wings and a tail. I began loading their bags into the aircraft: two bags in the nose baggage area just behind the engine, and the rest, including a case of whisky, behind the last two seats.

WOW, I thought, that's a lot of whisky, even for four guys!

Larry quickly climbed up on the wing, opened the door, and slid over into the left seat, the pilot's seat. "He must be late for something," I said to myself. As Larry's passengers were getting into the aircraft, a car loaded with four women drove up in a new caddie and parked just outside the fence.

"OH NO! They're here!" cried out the last passenger, who was standing on the wing, waiting his turn to get into the Cherokee. The Chinese fire drill now began. The one who was on the wing jumped off and hightailed it into the bathroom; the other three scrambled over each other trying to get out of the single door on the right side of the airplane, almost falling off the wing. One ran into Dick's office and hid under the desk, and the other two climbed into the backseat of two aircraft sitting in the back of the hangar.

"What is going on?" I asked out loud, but there wasn't anybody around to answer me.

As I walked into the lobby from the hangar with a perplexed look on my face, I asked Mickey, "What's going on?"

Mickey, who was standing by the aviation navigation map that was wallpapered to the wall behind the counter, advised me, "Better stay out of the way."

What did he mean by that, and why was he smiling?

I expected to see the police or FBI bust through the door, but it was worse. Four well-dressed women stormed into the lobby from the front door and stopped, looked me up and down, as if thinking, "So you're a male of the species too, huh." The largest one looked me in the eye and demanded, "Where are our husbands? We know they're here!"

I looked at Mickey for help, but he was now looking at the wall map as if he was plotting out a trip. My head snapped back toward the women. Flabbergasted, I responded, "I . . . I . . . I . . ." Realizing that I was innocent of any intrigue, they let me off the hook. Their steel gaze shot around like four radar screens looking for an enemy aircraft.

"We'll just wait for them," a petite sidekick to the ringleader replied in a voice intended to set me at ease. After about two minutes, the men realized that they were dead in the water and came out from hiding. I was scared and embarrassed for them. Their mommies caught them being naughty, and they were going to pay, big time. Without a word, they got their baggage out of the aircraft (except the case of whisky, that evidence was left behind), got into their car, and followed their wives to the execution site.

I turned to Mickey and said, "I'm never going to get married!" He just smiled.

My job wasn't without perils. Besides my normal duties, against Dick's whishes, I would hand prop aircraft that had a bad battery. I learned how to do this while working with Dale, since a low battery was a common occurrence with his aircraft.

On one cool fall morning, I pulled the Cherokee 150 (N6983W) out of the main hangar. A part-time flight instructor (who didn't have the pilot's swagger) had a lesson scheduled with a student. After their preflight, they climbed into the aircraft and went through their prestarting checklist. It didn't surprise me when they hit the starter, and the engine wouldn't turn over. It had been sitting in the back of the hangar for the last couple of weeks. I called out to the instructor that I'd prop it for them. He nodded OK. I walked to the front of the aircraft and positioned myself about a foot in front of the prop. "Mags off?" I called out.

"Mags off" was his response.

I grabbed hold of the base of the prop with each hand and pulled as if I was trying to pull it off the engine. This was to make sure the brakes were on. I didn't want it to run over me after it started. After confirming that the brakes were on, I put one hand higher up on one blade and the other hand on the opposite blade and, with a twisting motion, rotated the blades. This was a normal procedure that would loosen up the cold oil, making it easier to hand prop. On the second time pulling the blades through, the engine started. I was inches away from the rotating meat cleavers. I could feel the suction of the blades on my hair and pant legs. If I lost my balance, or if the airplane crept forward just a little,

I'd not only be dead but would have made a bloody mess of the entire ramp and side of the hangar. My arms were crossed in front of my chest, and I dared not move them. I took little baby steps backward until safe. My terror turned to rage as I walked around to the right side of the aircraft and climbed up on the wing to the awaiting open door. The flight instructor, in anticipation of my anger, just pointed to the magnetos. They were in the "off" position. There was a short in the mags, which automatically made them "hot." I climbed down off the wing and stormed into the office. As if looking for some form of ritual for when one has just narrowly escaped death, I bummed a cigarette and a match from a stranger who was standing there. I deserved one.

After going to work for Dick, I started flying his Cherokee 140. This was an easy airplane to fly since it had a nosewheel instead of a tail wheel. And after about twenty hours of instruction and solo flight, I was ready to take my FAA private pilot's check ride. "Browne," a pipeline pilot and designated FAA examiner who was based out of Midland, Texas, landed for fuel every Tuesday. On one particular Tuesday, he agreed to give me my check ride while he was on his fuel break. Browne had more hours than just about any pilot on the planet and had a reputation in West Texas as being tough on his check rides. That was OK by me. I was good, and I wanted to prove it to everyone.

The first part of the check ride was called "the oral." This was a series of questions to make sure that I had the book smarts. (That should have made me nervous right there – I only made a 70 percent on my FAA written test.) The oral started out OK, until he asked the second question. "Show me that the aircraft that we're going to use for the check ride was licensed."

I have never heard that term before, "Licensed?" I asked.

"Yes, licensed," he responded as if asking "Can't you hear, boy?"

Oh no, what does that mean? I thought to myself. Dread was starting to overtake my whole body. Oh no! The only thing I could think of was that a car has a license, maybe airplanes do too. So I took him to the tail of the Cherokee where there was a small one–inch-by-four-inch data plate with the aircraft info stamped on it and riveted to the tail of the fuselage. To this I pointed, hoping that I'd stumbled on the answer. He shook his head no, turned around, and marched back into the office where he proceeded to write me out a pink slip. I'd failed! I watched in disbelief as he climbed into his little Cessna 150, started the engine, and taxied off to continue flying his pipeline. I went into the bathroom and cried. My self-esteem, which has been almost nonexistent for my whole life, was just shot out of the sky. Then my lack of toughness caused me even more shame. Now I had to tell Dick, Ann, and my parents that I failed.

It turned out that "licensed" was not an official FAA term but merely slang to show that the aircraft had a current annual and one-hundred-hour inspection. Lesson learned; life and the FAA aren't fair.

At seventeen years of age, I went on to get my private pilot's certificate and at eighteen, my commercial pilot's certificate. Not bad for a poor kid who barely made it out of high school.

Being single and a pilot who had the keys to the hangar and Dick's aircraft had its advantages. Whenever I was off work and had the urge, I would pull an aircraft out and go flying.

I'd often go to a dance, meet some nice young girl, and ask them if they wanted to go flying. Of course, they would think that this was just a line, and it was. As if to call my bluff, they would respond with a "Sure, let's go flying." We'd then get in my brother's car that I borrowed, and off we'd go the airport. I'd pull a Cherokee out of the hangar and show them the lights of Hobbs. They may not have been impressed with me, but I was.

A number of times, I would fly across the state to Las Cruces and reestablish my relationship with Paula. Her dad was quite impressed with me. ("Marry that pilot!" I can see him saying.)

But time was running out for this, now that I was eighteen years old. I needed to advance my flying career and start making some money. However, I was about to receive another crushing blow to my ego.

Shortly after receiving my commercial pilot's certificate, I told Dick that I was ready to start flying for him. I could picture myself flying charters and actually getting paid for it.

"Sorry, Marc," he replied, in a not-so-fatherly manner. "Insurance requires that our pilots have one thousand hours of flying time. Anyway, you passed your commercial check ride because I told Browne that I wouldn't let you fly commercially anytime soon."

What? I knew that I didn't do that great on my commercial check ride. I don't even know why I went to Browne.

"Damn you and Browne," I said under my breath.

He had to notice my disappointment. I had all of 230 hours and spent all my money and even sold my guitar and amplifier to pay for aircraft rental. Renting aircraft for an additional 770 flying hours was impossible.

This has all been a waste of time and money, I thought. But as a good trooper, or rather a coward, I simply replied, "I hate insurance companies."

He said, "Yeah, I know."

It was now 1968; and up until my disappointment with Dick, I really didn't pay much attention to the war that was going on in Southeast Asia. That was until one night, while watching the news, I saw a CBS film report about a battle at Hill 55. This was someplace south of a place called Da Nang. They showed army Cobra helicopters making one gun run after another, firing their machine guns and rockets. Then a large army helicopter landed on top of the hill to pick up the wounded. That was really cool! I could do that, I thought to myself. But you have to have a college degree to be a military pilot, so that thought was quickly dismissed.

As required by law, I registered for the draft at the age of eighteen; and at my dad's insistence, I enrolled full-time at New Mexico Junior College. This lowered the odds of me being drafted. But after attending 13 different schools and with marginal grades at that, number 14 college just wasn't for me. I just wanted to fly. And once again, my grades showed it.

CHAPTER 6

The Army?

A bout once a month, a flight of army helicopters would land at Hobbs for fuel. They were being ferried from the Bell factory in Arlington, Texas, to the West Coast for shipment to Vietnam. While refueling one of the Hueys, I told the pilot about my desire to fly and asked about flying helicopters. He told me about the Army's Warrant Officer Flight Training program and that I didn't need a college degree! This was just what I needed, a way to fly and get paid for it. I guess my eight-year-old's grin showed him that this is just what I was looking for, because his attitude toward me changed. He actually started to harass me!

"Get me a quart of oil, now! Get that windshield cleaned; come on, let's go!"

I didn't know what he was doing, but I obeyed every order. As he climbed back into the pilot's seat, I stood there in my red coveralls waiting for his next command. He leaned over and said, "Kid, you're going to do just fine."

Excitedly, I told my dad about the Army's Warrant Officer's Flight Training Program; but to my surprise, this didn't go over too well with him. Since he was severely wounded in World War II, he'd seen what war was all about and didn't want me to go through what he went through. I already knew all that, but it seemed that flying a helicopter in Vietnam had him especially concerned. I guess the life expectancy of a helicopter pilot in Vietnam wasn't that good; in fact it was terrible. I ignored the statistics. The next day, Dad took me to a diner for a cup of coffee. Now my dad and I could always talk, but something was up; and I knew it. Aw great, I bet we're moving again.

As we sat in the booth sipping our coffee, he asked me about work and school. I gave him a stock answer, knowing that this wasn't what he brought me here for. He finally got to the point.

"Son, your mom and I like Paula; we like her a lot. And if you two wanted to get married, it's OK with us."

WOW! Was this my dad? I thought to myself, I'm only eighteen and just a gas boy. I have no money, no car, and I'm 770 hours away from being a professional pilot!

"Thanks, Dad, I'll give that some thought" was my reply. Now, I said my dad and I could talk, but that didn't mean that I listened.

I was still suffering from a chronic lack of self-esteem and wanted to prove to everyone that I was a man. To join the army and fight in a war seemed like a logical way to prove my manhood, especially if I could be an officer and a pilot. That would be so cool!

CHAPTER 7

Assertiveness

Some of the early maturer's advantage extends into adulthood. At thirty years, late maturers are still less confident, less settled, and have a poorer self-concept. However, they are also more assertive.

– I. P. Christensen

I went down to the local army recruiter and asked about the army's Warrant Officer's Flight Training Program. He briefed me on the battery of tests that I would have to take; and if I passed, then I would be guaranteed flight school. However, he went on to relate the disclaimer: "The washout rate is almost 50 percent. But if you do wash out, the army will help you choose another vocation."

Yeah, right. They will help me to be a foot soldier in Vietnam. I agreed to the terms. I might die in Vietnam, but I'd die a man.

The army paid for my bus ticket to Amarillo, which I thought was awful nice of them. There I took test after test. The day culminated with a panel interview with two men and a woman, all in real military uniforms. The woman, who was a captain, asked me, "What makes you think you could fly?"

I responded, "I can fly; I've got a commercial pilot's license."

I guess she wasn't allowed to be impressed with an eighteen-year-old commercial pilot because her response was "You know, helicopters are different than fixed-wing aircraft."

At this point, I thought humility would be the best plan. So I responded with my best West Texas drawl, "Yes, ma'am."

Either this worked or they were just hard up, because I received notice that I passed and was ordered to report to El Paso, Texas, where I would be inducted into the army.

Mom and dad were not thrilled at all about me joining the army. Every night on the news, there were reports about battles, helicopters being shot down, and the body count. For the first time, I was starting to realize the seriousness of my decision. This really hurt my parents. I'm sure that they felt they were going to lose their youngest son. Dad understood; he always does. Anyway, he did the same thing some twenty-five years earlier.

I was both excited and nervous. Am I doing the right thing? What if I fail? I'd be a ground troop in Vietnam! Oh well, I was about to get drafted anyway. At least I'd have a shot at flying.

Now another bus ride, this time to El Paso where I was sworn in. Good or bad, I was now in the army. I was put up at the YMCA, where the army paid for the $7 room. They paid too much. I came from a poor family, but I never stayed in anything like that. The next morning, I boarded a jet for Dallas, along with about a dozen other men (boys, really), who were inducted along with me. After landing, we deplaned into a blast of hot humidity that took my breath away. I'd never been anywhere like Dallas before and wondered if Vietnam would be like this. Gawd, I hope not, I thought. My fellow inductees all went different directions to gates that reflected the different branches of service we joined. There were no goodbyes, no bonding, nor did anyone want to be there. We were all wrapped up in our own wondering, "What have I just done?"

The gate to Fort Polk, Louisiana, was at the far end of the corridor. That should have told me something right there. No one in their right mind would want to go to Fort Polk. There were about twenty men, mostly boys my age, who were sitting anywhere they could find space. Some looked like they had been there for hours, lying in the corridor, trying to sleep. There was no laughing, no joking, and no one was singing "America the Beautiful."

I glanced around, but no one wanted to make eye contact with me. Man, these guys act like they just came from a funeral, I thought. That must have been the mood of them and their family when they left home. I didn't feel that way. I was going to fly. That is, after I get this boot camp crap out of the way.

After about an hour, we all boarded an old DC-3. This was a multiengine tail dragger that they used in World War II. Yeah, I could fly it. The cute little flight attendant, the only one, announced over the primitive intercom, "Welcome aboard Trans Texas Airlines . . . blah, blah, blah." But my ears perked up when she said, "Don't worry about all the noises, unless they stop, then worry." She was right about the noise. That old airplane creaked, rattled, and shook all the way to Fort Polk.

It was close to midnight when we arrived, and it was foggy. I'd never seen fog that bad, and I sure wouldn't fly in it. Those pilots were good.

No offense to those from Louisiana, but Fort Polk seemed to me to be the armpit of America. I didn't know there were towns like Leesville in this country. It was a dirty little town just outside the gates of Fort Polk that catered to the sleaziest desires of soldiers. One night when basic training was about over, I got a four-hour pass so I decided to tour Leesville. One hour is all I could take. My mama didn't tell me about places like that, but I was sure she wouldn't want me there.

Coming from New Mexico, I thought I knew heat; but July in the heart of Louisiana was a different story! The heat and humidity almost killed me. I mean that; I almost died. I suffered from a heat stroke. The army's solution to heat prostration was to give you multiple salt tablets. I did this every morning, and it seemed to work; but I wondered why so many people had heart attacks while in basic training.

I was six feet tall and weighed less than 150 pounds. I was hungry all the time. I heard that during basic training, if you need to lose weight you'd lose it; and if you needed to gain weight, you'd do that too. I wanted to gain weight. The problem was that I wasn't getting enough food. Oh, the food there was OK, but rarely did we get a second helping. A number of us were constantly hungry. The problem? One day while on KP, I watched the cook fill his trunk of his car with our food. He was stealing my food! But I dare not say anything for fear of reprisal.

I was elated to get the eight weeks of hell over with. Now, to get down to what all this suffering was really for, learning to fly helicopters. A busload of us left Fort Polk and headed for Fort Walters, located next to the small Texas town of Mineral Wells, just about sixty miles west of Fort Worth. I was assigned to the warrant officer's class of 69-15, which was to be the fifteenth class to graduate in 1969. Each flight company wore different colored hats, and we wore the brown hats. Fort Walters had a primary heliport just northeast of town and then another at the Mineral Wells Municipal Airport.

The advanced primary training facility, which was huge, was located about eight miles west of town. Then scattered all over a forty-mile radius were dozens of stage fields. At different times of the day, the three main locations looked like bees coming out of a beehive. There were helicopters everywhere. It was great! I couldn't wait to get to fly and for free!

I was eighteen, and the second youngest cadet in my company. That was until the youngest cadet washed out, then I was the youngest. I loved to fly, and it showed. I still had that eight-year-old's grin. My platoon flew the Bell OH-13, like the one used on the TV show *MASH*. In fact, one of the helicopters I flew was used in the Korean War. Most everyone else flew the Hughes TH-55. I guess it was a good helicopter, but I liked the OH-13. It just looked cool.

My instructor's name was Mr. George. He was from West Texas and was an ancient fifty years old. When he found out that I was from Hobbs, he requested me as one of his four students. I guess my weighing only 150 pounds helped since he was on the plump side, and the OH-13 couldn't carry much of a load. All the instructors had four students, which was more than they were able to care for; so one would end up washed out almost immediately and another down the road. I made the first cut, but then, I wasn't worried.

We learned everything there was to know about helicopters and being an officer. I already knew how to navigate, since it was the same navigation principles that I learned as a civilian. But I really needed to learn how to be an officer. I was raised a little on the sloppy side, and this was not tolerated in flight school. We even had a course in English. I guess I needed that too.

We lost one classmate during primary training when his helicopter crashed and rolled over on top of him. I'm sure that they told us what went wrong, but it didn't matter to me. I trusted the army to provide us the very best aircraft and training available; and in spite of the accident, I still felt that way. However, the accident had a negative effect on some of my fellow cadets. After the accident, the dropout rate increased. No sweat, just part of the game, I told myself. And anyway, it won't happen to me 'cause I'm good.

I was not only good; I was very good. I may have been the youngest cadet in my class, a fact that I didn't like but had a lifetime of getting used to; but I was also the first to go solo! I was the first to go solo not only in my platoon, but in the entire company, and with only eight hours of dual instruction at that! For the first time in my life, my peers respected me.

The presolo flight training was conducted at one of the many stage fields that were leased from local farmers. Ours was located northeast of Mineral Wells. There really wasn't much to them, just a small flight instructor's building adjacent to two rows of eight helipads used for parking and four larger pads just off the corners of the eight parking pads that were used for takeoff and landings. Here we learned to hover, take off, fly a traffic pattern that was similar to the one I used as a student back in Seminole, and land. This time to a concrete pad instead of a runway.

It was at one such stage field that Mr. George got out of the helicopter and said, "OK, Marc, take 'er around three times and then sit 'er down and wait for me. Remember, it's going to feel a lot lighter without me."

We had spent eight hours of training that included hovering and what seemed like endless takeoffs and landings, but was he actually going to solo me? I knew I was doing OK, but not good enough to go solo! I trusted Mr. George implicitly, so I responded with a confident, "Yes, sir." My takeoff was easy, and the rectangle-shaped traffic pattern was the same as what I learned from Dale back in my *Jenny*, only at a lower altitude. But as I made an approach to a hover, well, it was a little shaky. It was actually easier to hover with a heavy load than it was light. I couldn't help but wonder if Mr. George was watching and thinking that he made a mistake. The next takeoff, traffic pattern and approach to a hover was actually pretty good. OK, I know I can do it, I thought.

After my last approach instead of taking off, I was to put it on the ground. So I slowly started to lower the collective and reduce the throttle at the same time. She gently came down from a three-foot hover until the right skid hit the ground. Without Mr. George's weight, I was a little lopsided and was hovering with the right side lower than the left. So after the right skid hit, it bounced up causing the left skid to hit, and that bounced up and then the right again. It did this three or four times until I pulled the OH-13 back up to a hover in order to have a good talk with myself, "Come on, Marc, put 'er down like a pro," I said out loud. Gently, I lowered the collective while at the same time rolling the throttle off a little. This time, when the right skid touched the ground, I stopped and let the helicopter sit there with one skid on the ground and then slowly lowered the collective until the left skid touch; and without stopping, I continued to lower the collective until all the lift was out the rotor system, like air out of a parachute. I did it!

I looked over at the instructor's shack and saw Mr. George who was already walking back to my panting bird that was just sitting there at idle with the rotor blades singing, "I want to fly . . . I want to fly."

I was expecting an excited Mr. George to greet me with fireworks and slap on the back, but none of that. Maybe this is how the army does things; in a matter of fact way, he climbed in and said, "OK, I've got the controls." He rolled the throttle on and brought the rotor RPM back up and pulled the collective and up to a hover. After waiting our turn for takeoff, we headed back toward the Fort Walters primary base.

I wondered, Is he mad at me? Maybe he saw that last landing and was disappointed. No, it was nothing that shallow. Later in my training, another one of Mr. George's students and I would go over to his house for supper and drink. It turned out that many teachers who put so much of their life into training their students would form a bond with their students. He was forming a bond with me, but he knew the ramifications of my success – Vietnam.

On any given day, only one-third of the student pilots flew back to the base with the instructor, while the other students rode back in the bus. Since the OH-13 wasn't that fast, by the time we landed, tied down the rotor blades, completed the paperwork, and post-flight briefing, the bus would be there waiting for us. Normally, the bus would take us the half-mile trek to our barracks where our tack officer would be waiting for us with more fun and games in store. Today was different. I'd just soloed a helicopter. So the bus made a right turn out of Fort Walters and headed toward town. I knew where we were going, and my heart was pounding with excitement. Yep, we pulled into the Mineral Wells's Holiday Inn and parked in front of two helicopter rotor blades. They must have been from a Huey. These huge blades were standing on end, crossed at the top, and straddling the sidewalk that led to the motel swimming pool. My fellow cadets bodily extracted me from the bus, carried me past the rotor blades, and threw me into the cold water. It felt great! All my fellow students cheered me as I climbed out of the pool. Still dripping wet and with no towel, I climbed back into the bus amidst an assortment of slaps on the back and congratulations. WOW! To be accepted and even liked! The sign that was attached to those blades said "Through these blades passed the best helicopter pilots in the world." Yep, and I was one of them.

It seemed strange that I had such a hard time focusing in school, and my grades showed it. And almost anything distracted me whether from schoolwork or playing the guitar. But flying a helicopter was different. I was comfortable, at home in the cockpit. Come to think of it; flying a helicopter was nothing more than one big distraction. The pilot's attention had to be divided between so many distractions that it actually fit in quite well with my learning disabilities. How about that? I found something in which I actually had the advantage.

As a reward for being the first to go solo in the company, the company commander awarded me a three-day pass. I really didn't need or want one and even felt guilty that I wasn't exhausted and wanted to go home. But I guess the thing that was expected of me was to call Paula and my mom to let them know that on the following weekend, I had three days off. To my surprise, Paula took a bus to Hobbs where she hooked up with my mom and drove to Mineral Wells to see me. I felt bad that I didn't take the relationship with Paula as seriously as my parents and Paula did. I guess my mom and dad were still trying to get us married, but really, all I wanted to do was to fly helicopters. Although they didn't say anything, I think Paula and my mom were disappointed when they left Sunday morning. That made me feel even worse, not for my mom but for Paula. She really was a special girl, but I wasn't ready for a special girl. Damn! Everybody assumed that we were going to get married. I should have put a stop to it, and I didn't. This reminded me that I still had the hang-up of being a people pleaser. I just want people to like me. Instead of addressing the problem, I just ignored it and hoped it would go away. Not good. Oh well, I thought, maybe I'll be ready to marry her later.

The flying part of the Warrant Officer Flight Training program was a joy. I was in my element. But things weren't going so well back at the barracks. We had daily inspections. The tack officer would inspect our clothes, shoes, haircuts, cubicles, and beds, on and on. Now I wasn't the neatest person in the world. Actually, I was quite sloppy. My mom had always picked up after me. And to make things worse, I was assigned a roommate who was just as bad. We were constantly getting into trouble because my socks weren't lined up just right, or my bed wasn't tight enough. I was convinced that if it weren't for my flying, they would have washed me out of the program.

My classmates liked me all right, but they didn't take me very seriously. They treated me like I was their little brother. After so many years in school dealing with bullies, being a little brother didn't bother me at all. In fact, it was nice. Each cadet took their turn in being the platoon's candidate officer (CPO). The CPO would organize the students in behalf of our tack officer. On my first and only opportunity to show my leadership abilities in front of our tack officer, I marched up to the front of the students who were standing around waiting for me to take charge. With a crisp right face, I spun toward my fellow students and barked out "FALL IN!" Instead of lining up in a neat row at attention, "my men" rushed toward me, picked me up, and bodily carried me into our barracks where they commenced to remake my bed with me in it, to military standards, I must say. What disrespect! However, our tack officer thought it was hilarious.

Although the flying so far was most enjoyable, it really became fun when we transitioned to the advanced stage of our primary training. This involved flying cross-country, landing in confined areas, landing on pinnacles, and night flying. For this training, we were bussed daily out to the Advanced Training Facility that was located west of Mineral Wells. This was a modern aircraft maintenance and classroom facility that was flanked on the west and east side by what I guessed to be upward of a hundred helipads, and there was a helicopter parked on each one. From here, we would take off and fly to staging areas that were similar to the ones we used for our primary training, except these all had Vietnamese names, like Cam Lo and Phu Bi. We were told that they wanted us to get used to using Vietnamese names. Hmmm, I wonder why? We all knew where we were going. If we made it through flight school, we'd go as a pilot and if not, as a grunt, a foot soldier. This put our fun and games into a serious perspective. What we were learning would be put to use.

Mr. George was now out of the picture since he was a civilian-contracted instructor responsible for teaching us the basics. From here on out, our instructors would be army issued warrant officers. Every one of them came from Vietnam, which made them heroes in our eyes.

From the staging areas, we would depart on our cross-country training flights and later to the confined areas and pinnacles. Since I already knew how to navigate from my civilian training, this was little more than a review for me. However, landing in confined areas and on top of pinnacles was new and a real blast.

For most of this training, we worked out of a staging area called Dong How, which was located about ten miles south of the training center. I liked this area because there were ridgelines, pinnacles, rivers, and trees, like I imagined Vietnam to be.

After the initial checkout by our Instructor Pilot (IP), we would go off solo, looking for a confined area or pinnacle that had four white tires marking an approved landing site for students. Was this supposed to be this much fun?

So it was on one beautiful Texas morning, I was flying solo with the assigned mission to practice landing at confined areas and pinnacles. I'd just finished taking off from a pinnacle when I noticed a nice little confined area surrounded by mesquite trees. I've never seen this one before, and it looked challenging. So I flew over the LZ at five hundred feet above the ground, and yep, there were four white tires. I started to circle it like a lion circling its prey. I started the high recon by the book. First, I looked for other aircraft who may have wanted to land at the LZ at the same time. (Wouldn't want to collide with another aircraft while on approach; that would ruin our day.) Next, I checked the wind direction and mentally plotted an approach and departure path into and out of the LZ. I then descended to three hundred feet where I performed the low recon. I looked for wires, trees, and anything else that could get tangled up in my main rotor or tail rotor blades. Then like a child sliding down a playground slide, my bird slid down the imagined glide path that I plotted, clearing the trees and ending up at a three-foot hover. With a big grin on my face, I gently lowered the collective until the skids kissed the ground. Yeah, I'm good, I thought to myself.

Normally, I would immediately raise the collective and depart the LZ to go off and conquer another. But this time, I decided to roll the throttle back to idle, friction down the controls, and get out to take a look around. What if an IP flew over and saw me outside the aircraft taking a stroll? I'd just explain that I had to take a leak. He may still chew me out, but no one ever said we couldn't. Everything was OK until I rolled the throttle back to idle. I was still in the aircraft when the helicopter slowly rocked backward on the back heals of the skids. I felt the curved tubing that protected the tail rotor hit the ground and stayed there. I must have looked like Roy Rogers and his horse, Trigger, raring up.

"Wooo, this ain't right," I said out loud. I pushed forward on the cyclic, thinking that this would put the horse back on all four. But instead the rotor head started to bump into the mast. *Bam bam bam!* CRAP, I thought, mast bumping could cause the mast to snap off! Quickly, I returned the cyclic to the neutral position. Still sitting there looking up at the top of the trees, I knew I had a problem. My attention now went to my tail rotor. Was it hitting the dirt or rocks? That would ground me there for sure. So I frictioned down the controls and climbed out of my rocket ship. I took a couple of steps away from the machine, which looked so awkward, sitting on the heels of its skids with the blades whirling. I walked back to the tail rotor, which was singing, *whirrrr.* I'd never been this close to the tail rotor. I could see that the tail rotor guard was in the dirt but couldn't tell if the tail rotor had dug a hole or not. Not wanting to get too close, I got down on my hands and knees, just about a foot from the moving rotor. The dirt was fairly hard, and

I didn't see any evidence that the rotor had hit anything or dug a hole; but it was close, too close. I was no more than a half-inch away from washing out of the program. Now my thoughts turned to my bladder. I really didn't have to go that bad before, but now I really had to go. Anyway, I'd better validate my alibi and went over to a tree and watered it. Now I've got to do something, I thought, but what? I went back over to the stuck bird, which was still running, and climbed up on the front of the skids and hoped my weight would cause the helicopter to level. Nope, it didn't work. So I climbed back into the pilot's seat and strapped myself in. All the while the bird continued to grind as if saying, "You got me into this mess; now get me out!" I decided to try to get back into the same configuration that I was in before this unexpected maneuver occurred. Keeping the cyclic in the neutral position, I slowly rolled the throttle on to full RPM. Then, ever so slowly, I moved the cyclic forward. It worked! The helicopter slowly started to level itself. Once we were level, as if this never happened, I pulled pitch and flew out. I suppose I should have confessed this event to my instructor so everyone could learn from my mistake. NO WAY. I figured I was probably the only one this had ever happened to or ever would happen to, so I kept it to myself.

CHAPTER 8

Advanced Training

After the successful completion of the Army's Primary Flight Training program, it was off to Hunter Army Airfield in Savannah, Georgia, for the advanced training. We were given a week off before we had to report in. This gave me the opportunity to go to Albuquerque for my oldest brother's wedding.

Jeff's wedding was, well, a wedding. It was just a typical wedding, and I really couldn't have cared less about being there. It was nice to see my parents and grandparents again, and I knew I might never see them again. But I felt out of place. I love my brother, but this seven-day leave was a distraction. And Paula was there. She drove up from Las Cruces to see me. I wanted to go to Savannah, real bad.

After the wedding, I said goodbye to everyone. Paula and I then got into her Mercury Comet and drove back to Las Cruces where Wayne Johnson, a classmate, was to pick me up; and then we'd drive to Savannah together. It was a long, long three-hour drive to Las Cruces. I guess my attitude toward the wedding was showing, and it wasn't the reaction Paula was looking for. She wanted some indication on my part that we were going to get married, preferably before I went to Vietnam. Nope, none there. I never could hide how I felt. Oh well, maybe after I get back from Vietnam, I thought. I mean, should you get married because you feel guilty? If so, then we should have got married right then and there.

None too soon, I met my ride to Savannah. We took turns driving his new MGB. Didn't matter how cold it was; this was a sports car, and we drove with the top down. From this trip, I learned that I really like sports cars.

Upon arriving at Hunter Army Airfield, I checked in with the company clerk and was assigned a room and a roommate, Tom Dam. Just my luck, another roomy who was as sloppy as I was. Over the next three months, Tom and I became pretty good friends even though he didn't go out drinking with us. I guess it was because he was married. I respected him for that. If you're going to do something, do it right or don't do it at all. I wanted to party, and I did it right.

Our next phase of training consisted of twenty-five hours of instrument training in an OH-13. Unlike the vintage Korean War–era OH-13s I flew at Fort Walters, these were new and were equipped for instrument flight. I didn't care for the instrument training. I figured that helicopters were meant to fly low to the ground, not in the clouds. Anyway, what we all wanted was to get our hands on the Huey.

That day finally arrived. The Bell UH-1 Huey. We'd been studying everything about her in the classroom and knew her very well by the time we met. She was beautiful, and she flew like a dream. Having a turbine engine, the Huey didn't require the coordination of the throttle like the OH-13 and had all the power we needed.

During this phase of our twenty-five-hour checkout, we lost another classmate. While on final approach to the runway at Hunter Army Airfield, he had a tail rotor failure. The tail rotor and the ninety-degree gearbox completely left the helicopter, causing the Huey to pitch down. The pilot must have instinctively pulled the cyclic all the way back in an effort to level the ship, but instead, it caused the main rotor blades to come down and cut off the tail boom. The resulting crash killed the instructor and critically injured the cadet. He was through flying. That night, I helped box my classmate's belongings that would be sent to his home. I refused to dwell on the accident. I felt certain that there was going to be more; and if it involved me, then so be it.

Now the training turned tactical, simulating the type of flying we were to experience in Vietnam. The hours of formation flying was a challenge, requiring concentration. Even a brief lapse of concentration could cause the blades to hit the other aircraft tail or blades. Either would be fatal for everyone in both aircraft. But it was really cool flying in close formation with an aircraft that was so beautiful. Next came the contour flying. Oh, I really liked flying just above the trees. It reminded me of Dale dusting the crops back in Seminole. If he could just see me now, I thought, he would be so proud of me.

Although we still had inspections, and Tom and I were still falling short in the tidiness department, there really wasn't much chance of us washing out; so we would just stand there at attention and take our butt chewing. We also started to get the weekends off. But I had nowhere to go. All of my family was on the other side of the country, and they didn't have the time or the money to come see me. Anyway, I chose this course and knew that this would be part of the game.

One of my classmates, Kenny Osmond, whom I really didn't hang out with because he was married and spent his off time with his wife who lived in a trailer park, asked me to come over for supper. He said he'd like to introduce me to his wife's sister. That sounded better than hanging out with the guys and drinking beer, so I said, "Sure." I guess he felt sorry for a young single guy who was lonely. Nah, he was just trying to set me up.

Pat Turner was her name. She was a beautiful southern belle, a little younger than I was. We hit it off quite well. Pat lived with her parents in Cocoa Beach, Florida, and just a couple of blocks from the beach at that. I now had somewhere to go, but no car. So I bought a car from a student who had just graduated and was shipping out to Vietnam. Two hundred dollars in cash and $200 to be paid later. What a deal for a 1961 Sunbeam Alpine. A sports car! The ragtop was just that, ragged, but that didn't matter since I kept the top down all the time anyway. Now on almost every weekend, I'd get a pass and go see Pat. Her parents really liked me. Her dad actually told Pat, with me standing right there, "Better marry him before he gets away." I couldn't believe he said that. What a jerk, I thought. Trying to put pressure on Pat. Or was that meant for me? I liked Pat and we had fun together, but that moment was a wake-up call for me. Let's see . . . only three more weeks until I was to graduate and then off to Vietnam.

I'm on the top row fourth from the right

I finally graduated. Not only did I graduate, but I was on the commandant's list at that. I graduated in the top 10 percent of my class. Who would have thought that was possible? The goofball, the mouthy runt, Marc Williams was now a warrant officer and with army aviator's wings too! I asserted myself and earned the respect of the United States Army. And nobody gave it to me; I earned it! That day was a special day for me. I really wanted my parents to be there on that day, but they were still going through some tough times, now in El Paso.

What a shock! I had orders to go to Vietnam, of all places. I had a few weeks' leave before being shipped out, so I drove down to Cocoa Beach to see Pat one last time and then off to Las Cruces to see Paula. How do I get myself into these fixes? I wondered. They were both now expecting me to marry them when I got back. Oh well, I'll worry about that later, I told myself. Vietnam is a bigger concern right now. I spent my last week with my parents in El Paso. They were proud of me but also stressed, really stressed. Their neighbor, who was in the military, told them that the life expectancy of a helicopter pilot in Vietnam was not good. Thanks fella, you jerk. Looking back, I wish I had given my parents more time and even some money. They needed the money more than I did. Oh well, all I could think of was what I was about to face in Vietnam. My dad understood.

My dad and I the day I left for Vietnam

CHAPTER 9

Vietnam

Late bloomers . . . show greater insight.

– I. P. Christensen

My mom and dad took me to the airport where I was to take a flight to Oakland for processing. My leaving was hard for all of us, but it seemed especially hard on them. Dad said, "Son, keep your head down, and don't volunteer for any missions."

That must have been the motto when he was in the war. Actually, that wasn't bad advice and probably should have listened to him.

Mom and dad must have thought that they would never see me again alive. At that point, I really felt sorry for them.

Now I always felt sorry for them because of their financial plight, but this was different. There was a good chance that they may lose their youngest son in war. How would I feel if mom or dad was killed in an accident? It would devastate me. "OK, let's get this over with," I said to myself. We hugged and waved, and I promised each of them that I'd write; and then I got on the plane.

After spending a day at the military processing center in Oakland, most of which was spent in the officers' club getting smashed; about 180 of us boarded a DC-8 Stretch. Next stop was Vietnam. Well, actually the next stop was Anchorage, Alaska, for fuel and then nonstop to Cam Ranh Bay. Thirteen hours in a cramped seat next to the window, I pulled one over on the army though, I smuggled a pint of whiskey aboard. "What are they going to do, cut my hair and send me to Vietnam?" For the next twelve months, that was our motto for everything from insubordination to getting plastered, which for some reason went hand in hand. For as long as that pint of cheep whisky lasted, Allen Sodergren and I spiked our cokes; we were so cool. Allen was a classmate from Boston. Everybody else was acting like they were at a funeral. We were having a party. My goodness, the flight attendants were beautiful!

Our mood changed as the coastline of Vietnam started to appear on the horizon. The effects of the cheap whisky quickly faded. For the first time, the realization that I was about to set foot in a real country that is in the middle of a real war hit me full force. The DC-8 touched down and taxied up to the parking ramp. Now Allen and I joined the funeral march. As if to delay the inevitable, everyone slowly stood up, gathered their belongings, and started to deplane. At the top of the portable stairs, I looked out over the huge air force base. It was actually a beautiful July day, hot and humid, but not as bad as Fort Polk. Trying to be suave, I told a beautiful flight attendant at the bottom of the stairs, "I'll be right back." That was weak. Like she'd never heard that before.

I was ordered to report to the 282nd Assault Helicopter Company at Marble Mountain Airfield, which was located on the coast of the Indian Ocean, just east of Da Nang. Our call sign was "Black Cat." After a formal welcome by Major Webster, the company commander, I went through a couple of days of orientation, which was unbelievably boring. Then I got to do what I joined the army for, fly. At 0700 along with all of the other 282nd pilots based at the Marble Mountain Airfield, I reported to the briefing room. This was where we were to get our assignments, and the copilots would be paired up with an aircraft commander. The briefing room was everything that I imagined it would be. It was a large thirty-by-fifty-foot room with about fifty chairs facing a large map of our area of operations. In front of the map was a podium. Major Webster would get up in front of the pilots and brief them on what their missions were and what the security situation was.

I was very impressed with Major Webster; he was a lot older than me. He had to be in his midthirties. After I was in country just a couple of weeks, the 282nd was asked to participate in a campaign in which several insertions were to be made southwest of Da Nang. The story was that he felt it was too dangerous and wouldn't put his men in danger. The results were that another assault company took the mission and suffered terrible losses. I believed the report and subsequently liked and trusted Major Webster. Yeah, I'd follow him.

I began to fly an assortment of missions, mainly south of Marble Mountain, with a number of different aircraft commanders. We would resupply small outposts with food, ammunition, and the mail. We would bring new troops in and take out those that were going on R&R (rest and recuperation) or going home. So needless to say, the soldiers on the ground loved to see us land at their small base. I was really over my head. Everything was happening so fast, but I took consolation in the fact that the basic principles of flying were the same no matter where you go; and I still knew how to fly. Fortunately, the new guys were assigned to the aircraft commanders who had the most time in country. "I'm here to keep you from killing yourself" was their motto. We would take turns flying, except when it required special skills, which was basically any time other than when we flew straight and level; then the aircraft commander took the controls. It seemed strange that all during my short flying career that the aircraft I flew seemed real, like a person with a real personality. I would give them names like *Jenny*, talk to them, coax them, and even scold them. But these birds, the Hueys, were like our army flight instructors and now my aircraft commanders, distant, like machines. I still loved to fly them. Oh well, maybe after I get one of my own, that'll change.

My training didn't stop when I got out of the aircraft. After supper at the mess hall, most of the pilots would go to the officers' club for male bonding.

The club was actually quite nice. It had carpet, nice bar with stools, slot machines (that rarely paid off), and about twenty tables that formed a semicircle around a stage. It even had that stale-booze smell, like the pubs in Savannah. Ah, a little bit of home. At fifty cents a glass, I formed a liking for scotch whiskey. The pilots who have been in country a while would invite us new "Peter pilots" to sit with them, which was nice. Other than where we were from and what class did we graduate from, they really didn't want to know anything about us. And other than a "really?" or "then what did you do?" We weren't expected to talk much. The bonding consisted of listening to their war stories and buying them drinks. That's OK; I could live with that. So went the routine.

It was about midnight on one such night of training that after I went to bed I was awakened from a chemically induced coma by a huge explosion. I don't know if it was the shaking of the ground or the flow of adrenaline, but I was instantly on my feet and knew exactly what was happening. Almost simultaneously, the siren went off, signifying that we were under attack. Then another mortar round exploded; this one was even louder and closer. By the time I hit the door and made it to the entrance to the bomb shelter, another one hit, still closer. They are walking them up to us, I thought. I must have been slow because the shelter was already occupied by four other pilots. Another explosion occurred even closer, now just every few seconds; then someone asked, "Where's Simon?" My roommate, my roommate! Aw crap, I forgot all about him. At that moment, he came strolling into the bunker.

"Hey, Marc, how come you didn't wake me?"

"Wake you?" I responded. "How could you sleep through this?"

I was expecting a chastisement from my fellow pilots and Simon too, but instead there was nothing but quiet, a quiet fear and then another explosion. Wow, that one was close! Then the granddaddy hit, a rocket. It hit about fifty yards away but shook the ground like it landed right outside our door. This rocket was in a league of its own. Our bunker wouldn't even slow it down. We all just huddled in the bunker until the "all clear" siren wailed.

As I climbed out of the bunker, I couldn't help but shake my head and said, "Man, this is going to be a long war." No one answered.

After about a month in country of which all was spent flying out of Da Nang, I was assigned to go with Dan Seabold, a senior aircraft commander to Quang Tri. Quang Tri was a very old city just a few miles

Dan Seabold

south of the DMZ (demilitarized zone) and about eighty-five miles north of Da Nang. Our helicopter was assigned to the MACV, which was the American advisors to the South Vietnamese Army. At night, we kept the helicopter at a helicopter revetment that was located in the Quang Tri citadel. This was an ancient walled

fort in the middle of town. We'd drive a jeep back and forth to the MACV compound on the south side of town. This was where I would live for the next eight months.

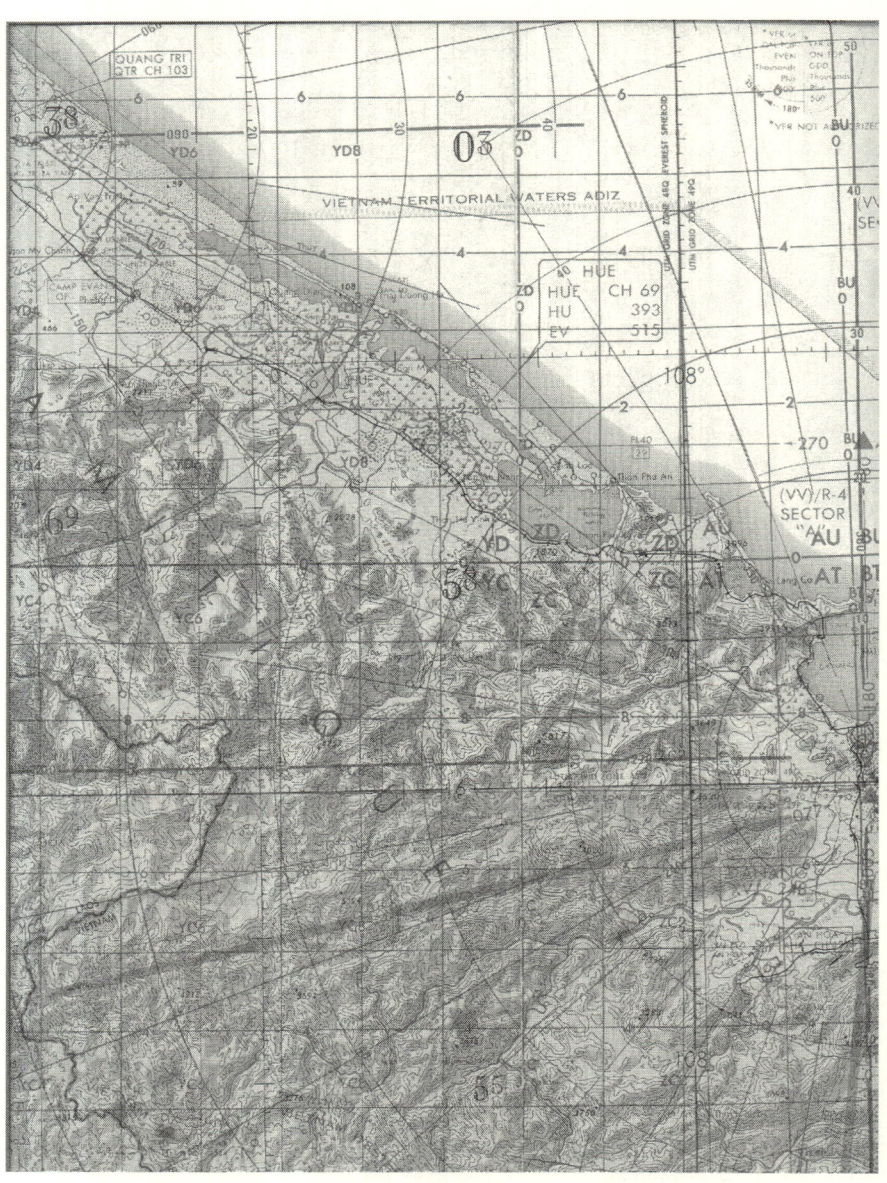

Quang Tri–At the top left and Da Nang–Bottom right

We flew single ship. That means that we didn't participate in the parade of fully loaded helicopters that would take soldiers, or "grunts," into some godforsaken jungle, just to get their butts shot off. No, every mission was different. On any given day, we'd resupply Long-Range Reconnaissance Patrols (LRRPs), sling load fuel oil to an outlying firebase, or fly reconnaissance missions looking for the bad guys. Since we were MACV's only helicopter north of Hue, we were also responsible for picking up the sick, the wounded, and the dead and taking them to either the ARVN (Army of the Republic of Vietnam) hospital, the morgue, or out to sea to the hospital ships, the USS *Sanctuary* or the USS *Repose*. But our bread and butter was taking Colonel Owens, Major Pierce, or Captain Peterson to the small villages that peppered the landscape from the ocean to the mountains, which were about twenty miles inland. Then once every couple of weeks, we would fly back to our home base at Marble Mountain to have maintenance performed on our helicopter.

On my first trip up north with Dan, he told me to just sit there and not to touch anything. OK, I can do that, I thought. We got a late start out of Marble Mountain, so it turned dark just after we passed a mountain pass called the Hai Van Pass, which was just northeast of Da Nang. On the north side of the mountain, nightfall was in full bloom. There were no lights. Either the villages didn't have any electricity, or everyone had turned off their lights so that the enemy couldn't locate them and lob mortars on them. I looked over at Dan, and he looked stressed. He was flying on the gauges, using the instruments to fly the aircraft. The weather was OK, except for a high overcast; but it was so dark that he couldn't see the horizon, and so he couldn't keep the helicopter level with an outside reference.

As we droned on, I felt as useless as a can of 3.2 beer. So I started to fiddle with the eyebrow light that was built into the magnetic compass that was located on my side of the instrument panel. It was actually quite neat. There was a little clasp that held a miniature lightbulb in place. I would slide the clasp off; the bulb and the little light would go off and then slide it back on, and the little light would shine again. After the third time I did this little trick, the entire instrument panel went black. I had shorted out the electrical system. Now it was really dark!

Dan yelled, "What the – did you do?"

Even though that was a rhetorical question, I stammered, "I was just . . ." Then I realized that I should be looking for the panel light's electrical circuit breaker that was somewhere in the rows of breakers located on the roof of the cockpit between us. Dan had already found it and pushed it in, and presto, the lights came back on. I was expecting to get chewed out, but instead he just shook his head.

I never did get to fly that night.

For the next month, Dan showed me the ropes, and then he went back to the States. Then Roger Kimmel, another senior pilot, took over. He wasn't near as serious as Dan. We would land on a sandbar on the Cau Viet River that flows through Quang Tri and wash the helicopter. Yeah, Roger was cool. And little by little, he would let me fly. I would even fly the complete mission, unless something scared him. This would entail landing on roads, on rice patties, or at a

Roger Kimmel's on the left

small MACV compound pad that was surrounded by a minefield. Roger gained confidence in my flying ability so much so that on one of his last trips back to Marble Mountain, he let me fly all the way back while he slept.

We flew missions all that day, so we got a late start on that flight back. It was completely dark by the time we got to the Hai Van Pass. But since there was a moon out, it was actually quite nice. Anyway, we could see the lights of Da Nang, which was quite beautiful, as we crossed the Hai Van Pass. Normally, we would fly low level around the beach so as to stay out of the way of Da Nang Main. That was a very large base used by the airlines and the air force. The aircraft that we were most concerned with was the F-4. A very fast fighter-bomber that took off toward the north over the beach and out over the bay. They would be heavily loaded when they took off, so they couldn't gain much altitude and expected everybody to stay out to their way, especially helicopters.

Roger was asleep, as were our crew chief and gunner. Since I was the only one awake, I had to make a decision. I decided to take a shortcut across the bay and stay at five hundred feet above the water. I know that's the altitude that the F-4s would be at after they took off, but I figured that I could see the Da Nang runway lights and would watch for traffic. If I did see an aircraft, I'd descend to just above the water. So as we trekked across the bay, I started to get nervous. This wasn't such a good idea. Oh well, I was committed now. I can't fly low level across the bay at light, I thought. I could easily hit the mast of a fishing boat that way. OK, I'd just watch the departure path for any F-4s. As we came in line with the Da Nang runway lights, I started to stare at the lights. All of a sudden, there appeared a red and green light right off our nose, about a quarter mile ahead of us heading straight at us and at our altitude.

I quickly threw the cyclic to the right, which caused the helicopter to enter a very steep right turn and lowered the collective, which aggravated the turn. We were about to go inverted, but I didn't take my eyes off the jet. But now, the red light started to descend, indicating that he matched my maneuver. "Damn, he's turning into us," I half yelled and half asked in disbelief. By now, Roger was wide-awake, and he grabbed the controls and pulled the Huey out of an aerobatic maneuver that the manufacturer of the helicopter, Bell, never meant for us to perform.

"What are you doing?" Roger asked. This time it wasn't a rhetorical question. I pointed to the jet that should have been screeching by us by now, but instead, the red light was now underneath the green light. Oh . . . it wasn't a jet at all, just two flares or Vietnamese fireworks that someone shot off. And it just so happened to line up on the runway lights like a jet.

To my surprise, Roger responded, "Well, I guess you thought that was an aircraft, and . . . well, I guess you did what you thought was right."

For Roger, that was a compliment. That episode didn't shake his confidence in me, but he decided to fly the last ten minutes of the flight into Marble Mountain.

CHAPTER 10

Nineteen-year-old

I'd been in the country for three months now, the last two of which were in Quang Tri. It was now time for my aircraft commander's check ride. The company scheduled me to take it during this maintenance layover. How about that? I thought. Roger gave me a good recommendation.

The check ride was scheduled for the next day, and it lasted the entire day. I was to fly with Pop Michaud, an old-timer who had quite a reputation and the respect of all the senior pilots, although I really didn't know him. The check ride consisted of flying company missions with Pop, south of Da Nang. That was the same area that I flew in during my first month in country. But this time, it was different. I knew what I was doing, and I wasn't in over my head. Although I didn't remember much about the area, I never had any doubts that I'd pass. It was just another day in paradise. Pop shook my hand and said I did fine. Coming from him, I guess I should have really been proud; but I didn't lack in that quality anymore.

My new call sign was "Black Cat 30." Yes, I was proud of it.

Black Cat 30

The next day, I gathered what would be my crew: Cecil, the crew chief; Gordy, the gunner; and Larry McCracken, my copilot. We flew back to Quang Tri. For the next six months, I was the man. I was to be the only aircraft commander for the Quang Tri MACV. Imagine that. At the age of nineteen, I was in charge of a very expensive helicopter and responsible for the lives of my crew, the passengers, and the mission. Yeah, I believed in getting the mission accomplished, but let's have fun flying while doing it was my attitude.

Cecil

Gordon standing guard

Larry giving candy to the kids

Our helicopter, the Bell UH-1 Huey, which I must say is the most beautiful machine ever built by man, was a marvel to watch. Cecil nicknamed our helicopter *Blivit*. I never did find out what *Blivit* actually meant. Likely, it was because it was on its second tour of duty in Vietnam and looked it. *Blivit* had a faded olive drab paint job and an assortment of patches scattered over its fuselage and tail boom. Like medals on an old warrior's chest, the patches covered bullet holes from previous battles lost. Cecil painted Coming Through on a three-foot inspection plate on the bottom of the helicopter. She wasn't new and shiny, but we were proud of her; and she was good to us. This large helicopter could hold about thirteen people (fewer Americans since they are larger); and for it to just sit there in a hover three feet above the ground, beating the air into submission, well, it was quite a sight that still impresses me. We were a team; no, more like family. It was Larry, Cecil, Gordy, *Blivit*, and me.

I continued to go through a metamorphous from being an insecure boy with low self-esteem who was obsessed with wanting people to like me, to a proud man who wanted people to respect me. Not necessarily because of my rank but because of my judgment and abilities.

For the eight months that I was assigned to Quang Tri, both as a copilot and now, aircraft commander, my crew and I lived at the MACV compound, which was about a city block long and wide. It was secured by the standard issue of Constantina wire, land mines, and sandbags. We actually didn't have it too bad. Not like some of the pilots who lived in tents out in the field. Ugh!

I shared a room with Larry, which wasn't that bad. You'd think that after spending the entire day together with me being the boss, we'd get on each other's nerves; but we didn't. Well, at least he didn't get on mine.

We didn't have an air conditioner, but we did have a fan, a small TV, and a hooch maid. She cleaned our room, polished our boots; and well, she was kind of cute. The compound had a mess hall that fed about forty people and an officers' club that sat about a dozen, plus the NCO bartender. Rarely were there more than a handful that frequented the small one-room bar, but I was a regular. I'm not sure if it was to help cope with the stress, dispel the loneliness, or to get a liquid sleeping aid; but most every night it was the same routine, scotch and water until 2200 (10:00 p.m.) and then one foot in front of the other until I made the twenty-yard trek to my bed. In the morning, I felt fine, no hangovers.

Larry and I were two teenagers without adult supervision. We had at our access a really neat flying machine, weapons, smoke grenades, and a life raft. What we could do with this combination was limited only by our imagination.

Once, we were sitting in our helicopter, waiting for a mission; and we were bored. Now, boredom was our biggest enemy. So everyone's eyes lit up when Larry came up with the idea of taping a couple of colored smoke grenades to our skids to fly around with. Anyway, it was almost Christmas. Now it was up to Cecil, our resident engineer, to figure out a way to make Larry's idea work. Cecil chose a red smoke grenade for the back of our left skid and a green one for the right skid. He then tied a string to the safety pin of each. I made the safety inspection to make sure that they wouldn't come undone and fly back into our tail rotor.

"Looks good to me," I said, "let's give it a shot."

Since it was Larry's idea, he had the controls when we took off from the MACV pad, which was located right outside our

MACV compound. When we were strategically centered over Quang Tri, Larry gave the orders for Cecil and Gordy to pull their strings. Just as Cecil designed it to happen, the pins were pulled, which allowed the firing spring to ignite the smoke. We then flew circles over Quang Tri, trailing a plume of red and green smoke. This had to look really cool from the ground, but I guess Colonel Owens, who was over MACV in northern Quang Tri Province and my boss, wasn't in the festive mood because when we picked him up later that day, he mumbled something about burning up his helicopter.

Although we were on standby seven days a week, dispatch didn't schedule routine missions for us on Sundays unless there was an emergency. This allowed us to sleep in and then get up and have lunch. Not being one to sit around and write letters back home, I gathered the crew and anyone else who wanted to go along, borrowed a jeep, and drove over to the citadel pad. And after a quick preflight, we'd take our own personal helicopter out for a spin. Our favorite hangout was out to where the Cau Viet River flowed into the Indian Ocean, where there was a navy installation. From this point south for about two miles, the beaches were considered secure. So we'd fly up and down the beach looking for just the right spot and then land. Sometimes, we would land next to a navy truck, which brought some sailors to the beach for R&R and see what they had to snack on. But most of the time, we had the beach to ourselves. At least that's what we hoped.

After shutting down, we would strip down to our Skivvies, break out the emergency life raft, and head for the water. I was always a little nervous that someone who didn't like us may be watching us, so a member of the crew always stayed with *Blivit* and close to the weapons. After a while, we'd get bored with swimming and playing in the waves so we'd break out the weapons: M60 machine guns, M16s, and .45-caliber pistols. My two favorites were a Thompson submachine gun and an M79 grenade launcher. We would then start "testing" our weapons. After we got the youth out of our system, we'd get dressed, go get fuel, and then put our toy away at the citadel pad. We'd get back to the compound just in time for supper, and then it was off to the officers' club.

CHAPTER 11

The Vietnamese People

I guess it was back in 1955, when I was about six years old, that I actually saw a black person. He happened to be gassing up his car at the Hilltop Service Station, which was located on Highway 36, just east of Marysville, Kansas. Marysville was a small farming community of about four thousand people, but not a single one of them was black. The only black person I'd ever seen was on TV, and my dad referred to them in the vernacular that was common at the time.

So I was quite pleased with my discovery. I was sitting in the backseat of our '50 Ford. As my mother approached our car after paying for the gas, I promptly leaned out the window, pointed at the man just a few feet away, and excitedly shouted, "Look, Mom, a nigger, a nigger!"

The black man seemed to take my indiscretion in stride, but my mother didn't. She was visibly upset and embarrassed. She sternly hushed me, pushed me back into the car, got in, and slammed her door. Off we went. One confused little boy and an embarrassed mother.

Mom didn't say much the rest of that day; but when my dad got home that night, she told him every detail of what happened at the Hilltop Service Station. Now my dad was actually a good man who was also my hero. He recognized that I was just a product of his prejudices, so he didn't discipline or even scold me. He did something better. He made me memorize a poem that I would never forget. "Every man is born alike in every place and nation and would remain the same except for wealth and education." Since my dad taught me that poem, I believed it; and in 1969, in Southeast Asia, I still believed it.

There's something about helicopters that fascinates kids, all kids, including the Vietnamese kids. Since I flew for MACV, we landed at most of the villages in the northern part of Quang Tri Province. This took in the area from just south of the DMZ all the way down to just north of Hue. It seemed like at every village where we would land, the schools must have declared a recess so that their students could come out to see us or rather the helicopter.

I'm still amazed how a large piece of metal can take off straight up, land straight down, and for it to just sit there levitating in a hover. Well, it was quite a sight that seemed to impressed the kids about as much as it impressed me.

As we approached a village, we would lower the collective, which would cause the big rotor blades of the Huey to sound out a *wop wop wop* . . . as if saying to everyone within five miles, "Hey, everybody, here come the Americans!" You couldn't sneak up on anybody in a Huey, that's for sure. The wopping of the rotor blades would announce to the children that a really neat flying machine was approaching their village, and they were in for an air show.

Of course, it would also awaken the enemy, Charlie, and notified them that we were coming. So Gordy and Cecil were always ready with their M60 machine guns just in case someone wanted to end the air show.

We operated close to the DMZ; and since the NVA (North Vietnamese Army) had antiaircraft guns on their side of the zone, our normal cruise altitude was all of ten to fifteen feet above the ground. Officially, this was to keep us from being a sitting duck. At least that was our excuse. The real reason was that it was a lot of fun for a couple of nineteen-year-olds to fly around so low that you had to gain altitude in order to get over a tree. So when approaching the village, we'd pull back on the cyclic just ever so slightly to climb over the trees then immediately lower the collective so as to not gain too much altitude and then back on the cyclic some more to begin our flare in order to slow down from our cruise speed of a blazing eighty knots (about ninety-two miles per hour). As we started to bleed our airspeed off to that of a slow walk, we'd push the cyclic forward and raise the collective until we were at a hover. We then gently lowered the collective as we felt our way down through the grass until we touched the ground. Once we were sure that we were on level ground and not sitting on a rock or booby trap, we lowered the collective all the way down then rolled the throttle off and began the two-minute cooldown. Cecil and Gordon would keep the kids away until the blades finally came to a stop. Then the kids were allowed to come and take a closer look at this amazing machine.

We heard a lot of stories about how bad the enemy was. One that was especially disturbing was the horror story about the Vietnamese kids who would be given a hand grenade by Charlie and then told to walk up to Americans, pull the pin, and then throw it at them, forcing the GIs to shoot the child, and no doubt with great remorse. I have little doubt that this actually happened somewhere; but I never experienced it, nor did anyone I'd  met, experience such a tragic event. But what we did experience was kids who were fascinated with our helicopter. Just kids, kids like those back in Marysville. They didn't throw rocks at us or make obscene gestures. They just smiled a lot and waved, with all fingers extended. I don't know, maybe I shouldn't have; but I'd even let them get right up inside the helicopter, in the pilot's seats.

Most of the children from the larger villages wore nice Vietnamese clothing while those from the smaller villages wore tattered clothing, but they all seemed happy. This was especially impressive since they'd known nothing but war for their entire lives.

They loved their games, loved to show off for us, and made us laugh; and we, them. Once we landed next to a village that had  a handmade walking bridge that crossed a river. They would grab each other's hat and throw it into the river, forcing the hatless boy to jump off the bridge to retrieve his hat. The more we laughed, the harder they tried to impress us. I can't help but remember the things that I used to do when I was their age, in order to get a laugh from my friends, like running around an elementary school naked at midnight. Oh, I really impressed them with that one!

One game we'd play with the village kids was to throw cartons of unwanted C-rations, which was about a third the size of a shoebox, to the other side of the Constantina wire. Constantina wire is barbed wire that is rolled into a coil. Two coils would be tied together, side-by-side, and then a third coil would be laid on top of the other two. This formed a barbed-wire wall with the purpose of keeping the bad guys out. While sitting in the helicopter waiting for our MACV advisors, we'd throw the boxes over the wire and watch the kids navigate through the wire as if it wasn't even there. The winner would grab the box and then return, without a scratch. Amazing! Not only could they perform this feat, but so could their older brothers, cousins, and uncles. This was very unnerving since it was the same type of barbed-wire wall that surrounded our MACV compound, in Quang Tri, keeping the bad guys out. How comforting!

My crew and I could speak just the standard allotment of Vietnamese, *dede mow* (get out of here) and *dinky dow* (crazy). I would point at Gordy and cry out, "Dinky dow!" This seemed to delight the kids as they'd point at Gordy, Cecil, or Larry, or whoever was the blunt of the joke, and laugh. But they seemed to especially like my turkey calls. You see, my grandfather, on my mom's side, used to own the biggest turkey ranch in the state of Kansas, the Silver Dollar Turkey Farm. And as kids, before we moved away, we would help out on the farm. They had turkeys everywhere, so we got to know them quite well. You'd chase them, and they would flee. If you'd stop and run away from them, they'd chase you. It's been said that everyone is a genius at something. Well, my claim to fame is my turkey calls. The turkeys would really talk to me when I called. So as the village kids gathered around our helicopter, I'd let loose with my best *gobble, gobble, gobble.* This was a real crowd-pleaser, resulting in a chorus of laughter, pointing at me, and replies in Vietnamese. Now from my limited knowledge of the language, it appeared that they were commenting on my remarkable intelligence and good looks.

One afternoon, we landed at a remote mountain village; and as we shut down, Cecil opened my door and slid back my armor plate. There they were, standing next to my opened door, two kids wearing old worn-out clothing, looking like  poster kids for Feed the Children Foundation.

One squatted in front of the helicopter and waved at me through the chin bubble, while the other stood on the grass next to my opened door, just inside the skid. He didn't say anything, and I was too tired to entertain him. We just stared at each other. Now we had big dragonflies back in Kansas, but the one that landed on the doorjamb belonged in a *Godzilla* movie! Both my new young friend and I looked at this small helicopter just sitting there, then back at each other. In a flash, as if we were in a race to see who could get to it first, he grabbed the dragonfly, crammed it into his mouth, and started chewing. Lunch! Ugh! He and his companion thought my disgust, which was vividly expressed by my facial expression and yelps, was most amusing, as they laughed and laughed. Evidently, I didn't know what a delicacy I was missing.

This routine of visiting villages was repeated numerous times in the infamous A Shau Valley. Every year, just before the beginning of the monsoons, the army would evacuate their positions in the A Shau

The A Shau Valley

Valley because they couldn't get air support. Then, after the rainy season ended, another bloodbath would take place as they fought to take this precious real estate back. Our job was to help evacuate the Montagnard villagers before the NVA (North Vietnamese Army) would begin their offensive. The NVA and the Montagnards didn't like each other. In fact, the Montagnards didn't even consider themselves to be of the same race as the NVA, although I couldn't see much difference. After making several trips back and forth to their village, we were quite familiar with their location and

Montagnard Village

didn't need smoke to mark the LZ. However, when the ARVNs (who were assigned to protect the Montagnards) heard us coming, they would have a soldier in the field to mark where they wanted us to land. This was to show us that the area was secure and clear of all booby traps and obstructions. It was normal to put the nose of the Huey right up to within a few feet of our guide. On one particular trip, I had the controls and was contour flying about ten feet above the ground as we worked our way toward the village. As I popped over a small hill, I saw a soldier standing in the middle of a small field next to the village and assumed that he was my point to aim at. However, as I flared the helicopter, I noticed that his back was to me; and as he heard the *wop wop wop* of our blades, he turned around. It became very evident that he was not guiding us in at all but rather, he was relieving his bladder. Larry and I thought that this was quite humorous. So while maintaining a three-foot hover, we just followed him as he took off running. All the while trying to put his equipment back in his pants. Our audience, his fellow soldiers, our MACV bosses, and the villagers, all thought that this was quite humorous.

Flying in the mountains of Vietnam was enjoyable, challenging, and very, very dangerous. The mountains were quite beautiful as were the valleys, like the A Shau Valley. The valleys were lush with green vegetation and blue rivers that cut a winding path through the mountains. But if we had mechanical problems, or if Charlie stuck his head out of a cave and fired off volleys of rounds at us, there was virtually nowhere to land or crash.

So if possible, instead of flying over the mountains and valleys, especially when going back and forth to Da Nang, we would fly feet wet (about a quarter mile offshore and one hundred to three hundred feet above the water). Then when we came upon the Hai Van Pass, if going south, or adjacent to Quang Tri if going north, we would transition back to our standard over land altitudes.

It was much less stressful flying feet wet. We didn't need to worry about someone shooting at us since we were out of the effective range of small arms fire. The only company we had that far offshore was the Vietnamese fishing boats, and we really didn't have to worry about them shooting at us. If there were bad guys floating around out there in a fishing boat, they certainly didn't want to advertise it by shooting at us. They were even more of a sitting duck (floating duck?) than we were.

If we had mechanical problems, we could most likely make to the soft white beaches. Even if the weather was bad, we would still fly along the beach but at ten to fifteen feet. It wasn't quite as safe as feet wet, but it was much better than flying over the land, mountains, and valleys. Anyway, flying along the beach, we could only take fire from one direction, to our landward side. Whereas, if we were over land, we could take fire from almost any direction.

This doesn't mean that flying over the beach or ocean was boring; it was far from it. The waters of the Indian Ocean were quite beautiful and relatively clear.

One day we were flying feet wet; and since Larry was flying, I was acting like a tourist, watching the fishing boats below us and thinking about what it would be like to live the life of a poor Vietnamese fisherman, when I was startled by something I saw in the water.

"What is that?" I called out over the intercom.

Cecil responded, "It's uh . . . uh . . . uh . . . uh . . . big fish!"

I asked Larry, trying not to hurt his feeling, "Let me have the controls just for a moment."

I shook the cyclic, and Larry responded with a wiggle. I made a steep, decelerating circle to the left and rolled out of the turn at a fast hover, one hundred feet above the ocean and the spot where we got a glimpse at the strange sea creature. There it was! I recognized it, a giant stingray. It was huge, as large as our Huey. We could see it flying just below the surface of the water, flapping its wings. I didn't know anything like this existed. We made a hovering turn, now down to about fifty feet above the water, and flew by it again, this time putting it on the other side of the aircraft so Larry and Gordy could see it. The chatter over the intercom wasn't about the war; this time the subject was a strange science fiction sea creature.

Gordy asked, "What do you want us to do? Evidently referencing to the fact that we just discovered something that warrants a call to a marine biologist. I don't know why I did it, but I authorized something that to this day I regret, "Go ahead and open fire."

Gordy pulled the trigger, and tracers began to work their way toward this rare creature and started to kick up small splashes of water. The stingray now made an emergency dive for deeper waters.

I immediately started to root for the stingray. Maybe Gordy missed, or the water slowed the bullets down; and the fish's thick skin stopped them. That was a bittersweet memory.

CHAPTER 12

MACV

Flying single ship for the MACV was actually quite challenging and a whole lot of fun, except when we were being shot at. Our area of operation went from the ocean, west past several mountain ranges up to Laos, and from the DMZ south to just north of Hue.

Since nineteen-year-olds get bored quite quickly, we had the reputation of accepting any mission. Yeah, I know, my dad said not to volunteer for any missions; but once again, I didn't listen.

I guess if I went to the daily briefings, I'd have been better informed about what to expect in the form of missions, but I didn't want to overanalyze all the details of what we were going to do or think and stress about all the possibilities. Well, frankly, they were just boring; and I would rather sleep in.

Typical was the morning we were waiting for a mission. My crew and I were sitting in our helicopter at the MACV compound pad, watching a water buffalo that was grazing in the grass about thirty yards behind our helicopter. Since Larry was from Texas, he thought he could ride that oversized cow.

"Hey, if those little kids can ride 'em, so can I," he confidently bragged.

What Larry was overlooking was the fact that these beasts were like family members to the Vietnamese families that owned them. Their kids were raised around them and loved these animals. It really was amazing to watch them interact with each other. The children would ride, play, and sleep on the back of these beasts; and the buffalos would obey their every command.

"Larry, you're going to get yourself killed," I told him, more as a legal disclaimer than in a sincere effort to dissuade him. He paid me no heed.

We followed Larry to the tail of the helicopter and watched him slowly stroll through the shin-high grass toward this mammoth animal with huge horns. I don't know, maybe Larry was a bull rider from San Antonio, but that thing had to be larger and uglier than anything Larry had ever ridden.

When Larry got to within about ten yards of the water buffalo, it raised its head, squared its body toward Larry, then lowered its head, and gave out a loud snort. That's all it took. "Every man for himself!" was the battle cry. Larry took off running back toward the helicopter while Cecil, Gordy, and I scurried to the roof of the helicopter. The bull took three or four steps toward Larry, as if he was going after him, then stopped. But Larry didn't look back and quickly joined us on top of our metal life raft. There we were, all four of us on top of *Blivit*.

That's when Captain Eugene Peterson drove up in his jeep and just sat there looking at us looking at the water buffalo who was looking at us.

"What are you, guys, doing?" Gene called out.

"Larry was going to ride that water buffalo and . . ." I stopped in midsentence, realizing that this story didn't sound real smart.

"Marc, those things . . ." Gene started in the tone of a father who was about to counsel his errant son, but he also stopped in midsentence. Instead, he said, "We need to go out about thirty miles southwest of here and pick up some POWs that a LRRP (Long-Range Reconnaissance Patrol) team came up with."

That was our briefing. We climbed down from the helicopter, slid into our military mind and gear, and then fired *Blivit* up. Gene climbed into the jump seat behind Larry and added to the briefing. "Marc, there's no LZ. They chopped down a couple of trees so you can hover close enough to load the POWs and their stuff. You won't be able to land."

"OK, sounds good," I replied then pulled pitch.

It took us about twenty minutes to get to the foothills of the mountain. Gene reached in front of Larry and pointed to a  canyon and yelled, "They're just under the south side of that canyon." He repeated the disclaimer, "They cut down some trees so you could hover close enough that they can load the POWs."

Trying to put the square peg in the square hole, I wondered, Why did he repeat that? Was he trying to tell me something, perhaps that I should be really concerned? True, they never taught us how to do this in flight school . . . Hmmm, if they captured some POWs there, could there be more VCs (Viet Cong) out there? Na, Gene wouldn't put us in that kind of danger, at least not intentionally.

From just above the north wall of the canyon, I could see the green smoke coming from the opposite side. The wind was gently blowing the smoke up the canyon from the lowlands, which was normal for this time of day. I radioed to the LRRP team, on an FM radio frequency that Gene gave Larry earlier.

"We've got green smoke."

"Roger, green smoke," replied the LRRP team.

I decided to make a tight left turn and set up the approach so that we would approach the LRRP team along the canyon wall heading east, into the wind. The canyon wall had a steep, rouged slope of about forty-five degrees.

"Keep your eyes open, guys," I announced to Cecil and Gordy, although I really didn't need to say anything. They already had their M60s locked and loaded.

When we were about the length of a football field away from our LZ, I started to slide the Huey down the side of the south rim and began a slow flare so that by the time we got to the LRRP team, there was no need to flare; and we ended up at a hover with our skids about three feet above the fallen trees. I knew that this was actually quite dangerous, but I loved it. I could feel the adrenaline pumping through my body. At that moment, there wasn't any other place I'd rather be and nothing else that I'd rather be doing. That is if we could pull this off.

I wished they'd have cut down a few more trees; our blades were awfully close to the trees that remained on the upward side of the canyon wall. The two LRRPs started to throw the POWs' gear on the helicopter and then helped the two captives climb up on the skids, and then Gene helped them to the canvas seats that faced the front, adjacent to Gordy's office.

I was focusing on holding the helicopter steady. The CG was changing as they loaded the aircraft, causing us to rock like someone standing up in a small boat. My ADD made sure that I didn't focus on one single thing outside of the aircraft. My eyes darted from the tree just to the right of our nose, to the river flowing down the canyon, to the tree just off our right side. Where I couldn't help but notice that these guys weren't tied up.

As I looked over to tree in front of us, I asked over the intercom, "Shouldn't somebody be pointing a gun at them or something?" Nobody responded. Gordy left his machine gun and was busy helping Gene get the POWs on board, and Cecil was scanning the area looking for hostiles.

"OK, that's it, let's go," Gene yelled out.

I had enough power to go straight up out of the canyon but thought that we would be an easy target as we came up over the ridgeline. Instead, I pulled the most I could, 105 percent torque. We started to move forward faster and faster along the side of the canyon wall; we then made a sharp turn to the left and, while in a steep left bank, flew right up next to the north wall of the canyon. Our airspeed was approaching sixty, now seventy knots, high enough to climb up out of the canyon and head back toward Quang Tri with our spoils. That takeoff had to really look cool from the ground. No doubt there were VCs, who were hiding and watching us. They must have been so impressed with what just happened that they forgot to shoot at us. Or more likely, they didn't want to take a chance and shoot their comrades.

I gave the controls to Larry and then turned and looked back at our two desperados. There sat two small men who, from the looks of them, must have been glad that the war was over for them. They looked really bad, not bad as in mean but bad as in scared, dirty, and undernourished. Even with all the wind swirling around the interior of *Blivit*, I could smell that they haven't had a bath in a long, long time. It was like BO that had soaked into their skin, and they never washed it off. That's the enemy? I thought.

"Gene, shouldn't you point a gun at them?"

"Na, they're OK," he replied with a smile.

Larry made the approach to the ARVN pad where there were several ARVNs waiting for us, with guns (finally). I watched closely as the ARVNs unloaded the POWs and their gear. I was curious about what the LRRPs threw on the aircraft.

Noticing a white block of clay, I asked, "Gene? Is that C-4 (a very powerful explosive)?"

"Yeah, but it's OK."

Everything was OK with Captain Peterson.

CHAPTER 13

Dread, Fear, and the Thin Line

The dictionary defines *dread* as "the fear of the presence or imminence of danger."

Helicopters were known for being sitting ducks. And the Huey was a huge (almost-sitting) duck with a cruising speed of eighty knots (ninety miles per hour); or if you were in a big hurry, you might get it up to ninety knots or 104 miles per hour. Now that may seem fast compared to a car; but for an aircraft, that's pretty slow. For most of the flying that we did in Quang Tri Province, we flew at ten to fifteen feet above the ground. After we got about ten miles south of Quang Tri, we'd fly either at ten to fifteen feet or at least one thousand five hundred feet above the ground, which was out of the effective range of small arms fire.

The army's rotor wing flight training is known as being the best in the world, but they never instructed us on what to do if you're "taking fire" at 1,500 feet, and especially if you're taking fire from something larger than "small arms," like a high-caliber machine gun. My guess is that as a sitting duck, there's nothing you can do but just hope they miss you or don't hit anything critical.

Fear and dread were keenly felt on an otherwise-uneventful day about forty five miles southwest of Quang Tri. We had just taken off from a mountain outpost with seven MACV personnel on board, a full load. And since we were already at our 1,500 feet immediately after liftoff, we just stayed there in route to a MACV base that was just north of Hue. About halfway through the thirty-mile flight, our left gunner opened fire with his M60 machine gun.

"We're taking fire!" he screamed over the intercom.

The enemy was firing on us with something bigger than small arms. I looked back and below us and saw what caused our return fire. Tracers were being walked up to us from our rear, so we wouldn't know that we were being fired upon until it was too late. Dread set in. I couldn't just hope we wouldn't get hit; we had to do something! I pulled the collective for as much power as possible and lowered the nose. This resulted in an increase in airspeed but a loss of altitude. I then started some short evasive turns, left, then back to the right, and then left again. I wondered if this would do any good. Just ten, maybe fifteen seconds was all we needed to get out of his range. Either that worked, or he was just a bad shot; either way, we dodged the bullet(s) again. But the fear and dread of an impending event took its toll on me. I didn't like being a sitting duck. I especially didn't like not being in control of the situation. So it was another night of scotch and water.

Although our helicopter was assigned to the MACV and the American advisors to the South Vietnamese Army, we would often be loaned to other outfits, including the CIA. This was the case on one clear, beautiful day when my crew and I were sitting in our helicopter at the MACV compound. Ted, a tall good-looking man in his late twenties, worked for the CIA. He was such a nice, polite man that he didn't fit the picture that I had of a CIA agent. Ted walked up to our helicopter in his civilian khakis and struck up a conversation.

"Sergeant Collins and I just got back from a long-range recon in which we came across an NVA (North Vietnamese Army) R&R (rest and recuperation) center, hospital, and rocket supply depot."

"Really? Where at?" was my response as if Ted was telling us a war story just to pass the time.

"Well, we know the general area of where we were, but we're not quite sure of our exact location; so I climbed a tree and tied my white T-shirt to the top to mark the exact location."

"Wow" was my response thinking that this guy was the real-life James Bond.

"Do you mind taking us out there and making one flyby so I can mark the location on my map?"

Boy, did I fall into this one! Let's see, Dad said never to volunteer for any missions. I think this is the one he was talking about, I thought as I looked at Larry and then Cecil.

Already knowing my response, he added, "They won't fire at you because they don't want to give away their position."

He wasn't ordering us to go; he didn't have that authority. He was actually asking us to volunteer. No matter. "Sure," I said. "We're full of fuel; just show us the way." Not much of a decision-making process here. Just overconfidence, arrogance, and just plain boredom – a bad combination. Anyway, Ted was with the CIA and a real nice guy!

Larry was at the controls. He pulled pitch and headed west across the first mountain range and then the second mountain range. My god, I thought, what did I get us into? I think we just left Vietnam! And with no cover! No gunship protection and no backup. Dispatch knew we were going west with Ted, but that's about all. If we went down, how could we tell anyone where we were? We didn't even know where we were.

I was sitting in the left seat, which was really the copilot's seat, but it had better visibility than the right one so that's where I parked my skinny butt. I turned and looked at Ted, who was sitting on the canvas seat just behind Larry.

I guess they taught mind reading at the CIA, 'cause with a map in one hand, he pointed with the other. "Straight ahead, it's just over that ridgeline."

Up ahead was a high plateau that was about three or four miles across and encircled by a fifty- to one-hundred-foot-high rock/jungle lip. I nodded. Just one pass was all I'd give him; we were taught never to pass over the same spot twice, for obvious reasons. The first pass would wake the enemy up, and the second would give them something to do, shoot down an American helicopter.

As we came upon the ridgeline, I told Larry "I've got it" and wiggled the controls, which was the signal that he could let go. I lowered the collective and the nose of the aircraft at the same time with the intent of passing just over the lip of the plateau, doing about ninety knots, all the while wondering if Ted could even see his shirt at this low altitude and speed.

My answer came soon enough, "I know where we are, just need to make one more pass," he shouted.

Oh boy . . . I know better than this, but he did assure me that they wouldn't shoot at us; maybe if I flew along the ridgeline and then cut in at a ninety-degree angle, we could get away with it.

As we flew across the plateau at treetop level, I looked out my side window and saw something I didn't see on the first pass. Oh my! I thought to myself. There's a lot of activity out there; this must be the right place. So I was surprised when Ted shouted for one more pass, just to make sure.

At this point, my desire to please Ted overshadowed my good judgment. Still talking to myself, I said, "If I cut another angle at forty-five degrees this time, I think I can get away with it and then pop over the ridgeline and get back home." So as we reached the lip on the far side of the plateau, I pulled back on the cyclic and raised the collective and entered into a steep climb. Then when our airspeed was down to just under forty knots, I pressed the right pedal hard. This caused the helicopter to make a sharp turn to the right with the nose pointed toward the ground in a dive. Now we were heading back in the opposite direction, just like the turns Dale used to make when crop dusting back in West Texas. He'd be proud of me.

"OK, this is it!" I yelled out. I didn't have to tell Cecil and Gordy to be ready with their M60s. Crap! I blew it! It sounded like someone was hitting the back of my helmet with a hammer. *BOOM BOOM BOOM* . . . Instinctively, both gunners opened fire with their machine guns. Oh shit! They're shooting at us, and we have no cover; gotta get to the ridgeline! I scrunched down, trying to hide behind the armor plating and fly at the same time. But with the size of that gun, any hit at all would bring us down! Oh! Fear and dread reigned for fifteen seconds. What am I doing here? We gotta get to the ridgeline, just a few more seconds. We made it! As we went over the rocks, I lowered the nose to stay below the sights of that gun. When it became clear that we again dodged the bullets, literally, we pulled out our cigarettes and lit up. No one said a word. We didn't have to. We all knew what had just happened. I knew we didn't take a hit; we were still flying. Larry, Cecil, Gordy, and *Blivit* had to be mad at me. I almost got them killed.

I thought, Hey, this is war, and we're suppose to try and win, aren't we? I still felt bad.

On the way back, Ted leaned forward and yelled that he'd like to land down there, pointing to over my shoulder to my eleven o'clock position. He then yelled the FM frequency to Larry, who wrote it down with his grease pencil on the Plexiglas window. Larry then called for smoke. We landed to a green smoke. A company of American soldiers had already cleared out of the tall bamboo like vegetation, an area large enough for several helicopters. Evidently, we weren't the first helicopter to land there. Ted said the area was secured, so we shut down. He went off to talk to one of the officers. Must be a field-grade officer that's over the area where we just got fired upon. I walked around the area for a few minutes, thinking, I'd still rather be in the air, even as a sitting duck, than down here with these guys. I can't see down here.

That night, Ted or the officer on the ground called in a B-52 air strike on the area. Then, within a couple days, the 101st Airborne Division swept through that area. They captured one person who happened to be the gunner of an antiaircraft gun. Ted didn't tell us anything about an antiaircraft gun. That would have been useful information. The NVA gunner had logged in his notebook that a helicopter flew overhead on that day, and he fired so many rounds at it. That was us! The B-52 air strike was close but didn't hit the target. But it was close enough that they decided that the Americans knew where they were, so they began to evacuate the area. Ted assured me and my crew that he didn't know about the antiaircraft gun. This was the type of gun that could bring down fast-moving, fixed-wing aircraft; but on that day, it had trouble hitting a sitting duck.

With the aid of scotch and water, I would analyze and scrutinize my decision-making process. Was pride, overconfidence, boredom, and the desire to please people influencing my decisions? All these are terrible emotions that kill good pilots and their crew. We had no business being there. By passing over the same area, not just twice, but three times, I had ignored the training that I received. I was not ordered on that mission and didn't have all the facts, facts that were needed in order to make the proper decision. Very poor judgment indeed. It was so dumb that if the CIA reported what took place, which they wouldn't, we would have all received medals. Well, maybe he did turn us in to the ARVNs.

Cecil and I receiving the Vietnamese Cross of Gallantry

I was constantly concerned about the enemy and our being shot at. Actually, a more deadly enemy was having an accident, to crash and burn. Of all my classmates and pilots that I knew who died, half of them died not from being shot down but from accidents. Weather was a major cause.

I learned that there's a very thin line between a close call and an accident.

It was time to ferry *Blivit* back to Marble Mountain for maintenance, and the weather was deteriorating. We couldn't fly feet wet because the visibility was too low. We needed to keep the beach in sight since it was our only navigational reference. So I opted for flying low level over the beach. The visibility was about half a mile. I maintained eighty knots of airspeed, which was much too fast for this low of visibility; but I was concerned that if we flew any slower, we would be tempting of a target for Charlie. If I was the enemy and saw a slow-flying helicopter right in front of me, I wouldn't be able to resist the urge to shoot at it. So the airspeed stayed at eighty knots.

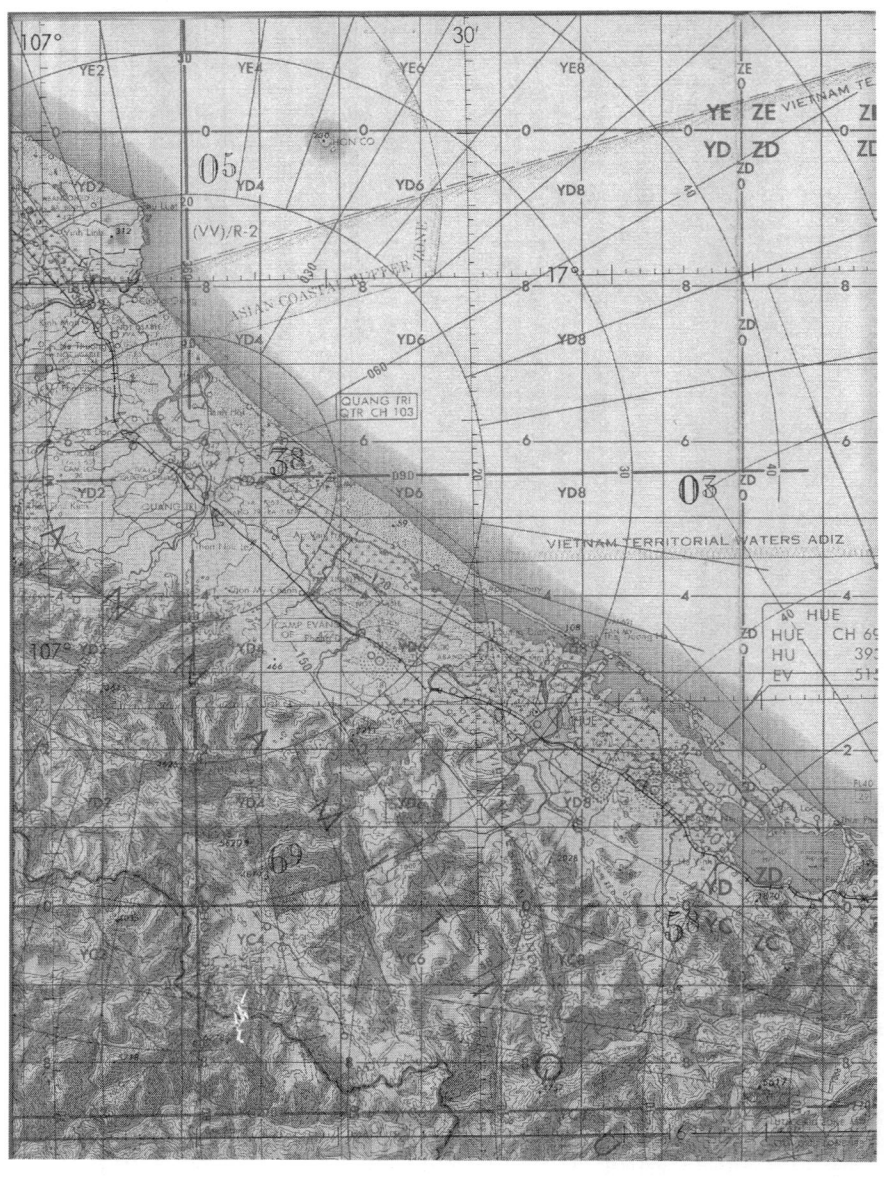

We then hit the reason why we should have slowed down. The inlet where the Perfume River emptied into the ocean was fogged in. We went IFR at twenty feet above the water. Our windshield was white. I looked down at my chin bubble, and I could see the water, which was being whipped up by the wind. We're in trouble, big trouble. I wanted to pull up into the fog, but we were just under the approach path of Hue. A constant flow of jets would be just over our heads. Plus if we go IRF, where would we go? What heading would we take? The ocean was socked in; and if we headed west toward Hue, we would be flying toward the airbase. And if we took up a heading back toward Quang Tri, we would be heading toward the radio towers.

With an urgent tone in his voice, Cecil called out over the intercom, "You're going to hit . . . Bank right!"

Hmmm, he didn't stutter; he really must be scared.

I had already started a slow deceleration, and now I started to bank just a little to the right while watching the water through my chin bubble. Any major movements with the cyclic, forward, backward, left, or right, would almost certainly cause the rotor blades to hit the water; and we would all die.

Waves in the chin bubble. That was my reference, my horizon that would keep us level, that would keep us from hitting the water. Good or bad, smart or dumb, I put all our chips, our lives, into this decision. I couldn't look up at our attitude indicator or look for a compass heading. At this altitude and airspeed, any deviation, which is almost certain to occur when you change from using outside references to the instruments, would be disastrous. Other than Cecil's exclamation, no one said a word. Do they know that we're in deep trouble? Maybe they're just maintaining radio silence so that I can figure a way out of this, and they didn't want to distract me.

At any rate, we inadvertently turned too far to the right; now we were over the bay and still in the fog. If I would have maintained my heading, we likely have made it to the opposite side of the Perfume River where the fog may not have been as bad. But then again, I knew this area and this inlet. There were tall trees on the other side, next to *Pistol Pete*, a small navy barge and gunboat base. So the right turn was correct. How thick was the fog? I didn't know.

Once again, I was lucky. The wind that was whipping up the water was blowing from the west and blowing the fog out to sea. After ten to fifteen seconds of unbelievable stress, the type of stress where you know that you may die, we broke out of the fog. We were over the bay looking at a radio tower a quarter of a mile in front of us on the west bank of the bay. We made a left turn and continued our trek toward Da Nang, but this time over the land.

That night, I had my standard debriefing with my confidants, scotch and water, and analyzed the flight. It's true that we didn't have an accident, but that didn't mean that it was a good, safe flight; and it sure didn't mean that my decisions were correct. I never did believe in the slogan "Any landing that you can walk away from is a good landing."

I remembered back to when I was working at Marshall Aviation, and Mickey Monk was my flight instructor. He said, "Marc, always have a way out."

After going IFR at twenty feet, eighty knots, and with no way out, I decided that one way out wasn't good enough; from now on, I'm going to have two ways out.

CHAPTER 14

Thirteen Days

In the book *Excess Baggage,* Dr. Judith Sills makes this observation about friendship. "The glue in most of your relationships, whether romantic or platonic, is a common interest."

This was especially true between Larry, Captain Peterson, and me.

Larry was a likeable guy from San Antonio and was about my age. We got along well, and he never questioned my decisions or authority, which frankly I would have if I were him.

Captain Eugene "Gene" Peterson, or I just called him Gene, unless someone else was around; and then it was Capt'n. He was a good-looking tall guy from Oklahoma. His assignment was to keep the village chiefs loyal to the South Vietnamese government. We got to know him quite well for almost every day he'd requested our helicopter for a mission. He took a liking to Larry and I, probably because he washed out of the army's helicopter flight school; and he still wanted to fly. There's a special bond between pilots and those who want to be pilots; that is, if the pilot likes the wannabe. Arrogant? Yeah, a little, but that's the pecking order. So Larry and I invited him into our pilots' inner circle. During the day, we flew him from village to village. And then at night, we would occasionally meet at the officers' club to have a drink, talk about buying a helicopter, and going into business together in Tucson, Arizona. The more we drank, the bigger the operation was going to be. There was no way in hell that we could pull it off, but it felt good to have the same dreams and with a good friend too. I had very few friends growing up, especially any that respected me.

After a couple of months, Larry and I noticed that Gene started to act a little strange. We would land at the outskirts of a village. He'd then go into the village without carrying a weapon, not even a pistol. The normal issue for an officer was a .45-caliber handgun and an M16 rifle. He said that he was just trying to show the locals that he trusted them. That was dumb! And we told him so too.

"Aw," he'd reply in an Oklahoma drawl, "it's safe out here."

"Gene, you've got a wife and two kids! Get your weapons!" was our reply.

November 12, 1969 was a crappy, gray overcast day. The depressing type that you just wanted to get over with. Gene requested the helicopter so that he and a couple of his men could meet up with a platoon of ARVNs and sweep through an area just off the coast and a little south of the Cau Viet River, which ran through Quang Tri out to the ocean. This was a routine maneuver that usually flushed out a few North Vietnamese soldiers that had set up housekeeping in the sand dunes. We'd done this many times before, and it wasn't without its risks. But it was always fun to fly Gene around. We were a team.

As we approached the general area, Gene, who was seated in a canvas seat behind Larry, which faced the right side of the helicopter, leaned around my armor-plated seat and pointed to where the ARVNs were located. I nodded, called the platoon on the FM radio, and called for a smoke. We could see the smoke about a quarter of a mile in front of us, so I called back on the radio that I had a green smoke. In broken English, the ARVN soldier said, "Yes, green smoke." I think if I'd said purple smoke, he would have responded with "Yes, purple smoke." So we just assumed that it was the right guys and not Charlie that popped the smoke. We dropped off four men, including Capt'n Peterson, who, to Larry's and my relief, was carrying the normal allotment of weapons.

We lifted off with Larry at the controls and headed back to Quang Tri Main for fuel. Quang Tri Main was a fair-sized army base just a little north of Quang Tri. After hot refueling, Larry took us back to the MACV helipad for lunch. Larry gently touched Blivit's skids down on the pad, lowered the collective, and started the two-minute cooldown. During that cooldown, Cecil and Gordy started the process that they've repeated a hundred times before. The crew chief would open the aircraft commander's door and slide back the side armor, and the gunner would do the same for the copilot.

It was during the cooldown period that the FM radio crackled, "Black Cat 30, Captain Peterson has been hit; we need you to come back ASAP and pick him up."

As if this had occurred a hundred times before, without a word, the open door procedure was quickly reversed; engine spooled up, and we pulled pitch. We were off the ground within seconds of the radio call, but this time I was at the controls; and I pushed *Blivit* faster and harder than we were allowed.

"Mr . . . . Mr . . . . Mr . . . . Williams," Cecil, our crew chief, who had a stuttering problem, called out over the intercom, "the . . . the tail, it's . . . it's going back and forth; we're going too fast!"

I ignored Cecil. All I could think of was that we had to get there before it was too late. My mind was racing. Hit? What did they mean that he'd been hit? Was he dead? Was there a firefight going on? Didn't matter, we were going in to pick Gene up. Fear was now starting to crawl up my throat, the feeling you get when you're about to start crying.

Other than Cecil's concern about the tail, no one said a word. We knew that this was bad. Although no smoke was needed, they popped one anyway. I didn't respond to the yellow smoke on the radio. I didn't want to talk to them. They may tell us something that we didn't want to hear. Before the skids could settle in the sand, Cecil jumped out to go see what his condition was. After just a few seconds, he came running to my door and yelled, "Cap . . . Cap . . . Captain Peterson, he's dead!"

"Dead?" I asked.

"Yes . . . yes . . . yes, sir."

OK, this is war, and this is what happens in war; let's keep it together, I thought to myself.

Damn, we had no body bag!

"Use the emergency life raft and wrap him in it," I yelled. I could see his limp body being wrapped in the same life raft that we used to play in the ocean. Gordy, Cecil, and Gene's three companions carried Gene over to the right side of the helicopter. As they slid him into the helicopter, his head fell back and hit the edge of the floor hard.

"Come on, guys," I yelled out, "I know he's dead but . . ." They felt bad enough; why'd I say that?

We took off and headed straight for the morgue. No one said a word until I called to Cecil over the intercom.

"What happened?"

"They . . . they . . . they said he was killed by, by, by a hand grenade."

"How, who, if . . . ?" I asked, but not expecting an answer.

"I . . . I . . . I don't know, sir, that's all . . . all . . . all they told me," Cecil stuttered.

As we started to flare the helicopter for a touchdown at the morgue's pad, I told my crew over the intercom, as if I were complaining that this wasn't fair, "You know he was to go home to a wife and two kids in thirteen days!" No one said anything.

Coming out of the morgue's helipad, Larry had the controls. We were all rattled. I felt weak physically and emotionally. I needed a scotch. As he pulled the collective for our departure over the Consantina wire, I saw that the torque gauge was reading 110 percent and still going up. I pointed to the gauge, and Larry immediately lowered the collective to bring the readings within limits. I put the intercom on PVT so that what I had to say would be between Larry and myself.

"Larry, we need to focus on what we're doing, or we'll end up like Gene."

"Yeah, you're right," he responded.

We continued to fly the missions scheduled for us the rest of the day, but no one's heart was in it.

That night, after supper at the mess hall, I went to my hooch but was only there for a minute. I thought of writing a letter to my folks back home, but I wasn't in the mood. So as I strolled out of our hooch, I mumbled to Larry, "Going to the club." I don't know if Larry answered me or not, but it didn't matter. I was finally going to get that scotch that I've been wanting all day then try to make sense of what just happened.

I walked into the club and made the required right turn in order to walk the ten steps to the small bar where the bartender, upon noticing my entrance, began to prepare my scotch. I paid for my liquid stress reliever, mumbled thanks to the bartender, and out of politeness turned and nodded to Dr. Fitzpatrick, who was nursing a beer just to my right. The bar was big enough for about four people to belly up to. But tonight we had it to ourselves. I didn't intend to enter into a conversation. I just craved some soul-searching and my scotch. Dr. Fitzpatrick was an Australian major who was our compound physician. He didn't frequent the officers' club very often, which was evidenced by his drinking a 3.2 beer; so I didn't really know him that well.

"Too bad about Captain Peterson; he was going home in thirteen days to a wife and two kids," I said. I guess I'm going to talk to someone after all. Oh well.

He replied in a clear statement of fact, "He wasn't going home."

I countered, "You don't understand; he was going home in thirteen days to a wife and two kids." My goodness, Doc, can't you hear? I thought.

Almost irritated, he stated again clearly, "No, *you* don't understand; he wasn't going home; he had an incurable venereal disease. He committed suicide."

Since I was working on my first scotch and water, I knew that I wasn't drunk.

"Suicide?" I asked.

Realizing that I finally was catching on, he calmly explained, "He laid a hand grenade down by an unexploded shell, as if to destroy it so no one would accidentally step on it; pulled the pin and then took three steps; turned around; and it killed him instantly."

I couldn't believe it! Gene killed himself! In a war, no one kills themselves; they kill the enemy and the enemy kills them, but no one kills themselves. But maybe that explained his unusual behavior of not carrying a weapon. He wanted to be "killed in action"?

I was distressed by what I was hearing, but I had to know more. "But if he couldn't go home, where . . ."

"Let me just say that he wasn't going home, ever," he said.

He acted uncomfortable like he didn't want to talk to me anymore; and frankly, I heard more than I wanted to hear. He must have noticed that I was distressed. He put his hand on my shoulder, nodded and turned around and walked out of my mental ward.

I sat down at one of the tables next to the bar. I just wanted to be alone with my thoughts. I said to myself (or out loud, I don't remember), "Black VD?" I remembered the senior pilots back at Marble Mountain would talk about an incurable venereal disease.

"You, guys, better be careful, or you'll never go home," they would counsel. "You'll end up on Hon Loa."

Hon Loa was an island just south of Da Nang where one side of the island was used for rest and recreation, and the other side was a compound that was off-limits. That was where they supposedly sent soldiers with the Black VD until they die.

I thought they were just pulling my leg, I mean you couldn't believe half of their war stories; why should I believe that the NVA would give the dreaded disease to young girls and then send them south to be friendly with the American GIs? And then there was the other compound that I heard about somewhere in the Philippines . . .

I signaled for another scotch. I wondered why their families don't bring them home for treatment. Maybe the government won't let them go home. After all, they couldn't afford to have American soldiers coming home and spreading some incurable venereal disease across America.

Still talking to myself, I continued, OK, if Gene didn't commit suicide, where would he go if not home? Then it hit me, missing in action (MIAs). If the government told my parents that I had the Black VD and couldn't come home, ever, my dad would stop at nothing to bring me home; I mean nothing. Classifying them as MIAs was the only solution. No wonder Gene committed suicide. Poor guy. His wife and two kids should be getting the news about now. I wished I could cry, but for some reason I couldn't.

Then as if someone just emptied my scotch and water in my lap, I sat straight up from my slouch. "My god, I've been sexually active!" (Although I didn't use such polite terms.) Could that happen to me? What would I do, commit suicide too? What if Mom and Dad got a letter from the army that said that I was a MIA? Oh, no, no, no! What if . . . ?

I wasn't the same after that night. My carefree eight-year-old's grin was gone. I carried this tragedy with me. Every time I thought of Gene, my thoughts would bounce over to me. Had I dodged the bullet? I started to look at my urine. Come on, who looks at their urine when they're taking a leak? Now I did.

What's that white stuff? Is that puss? *Oh shit!* I'm dead; I'm not going home! I can't believe it! I get shot at by everything that Charlie has in his arsenal, but I get killed by a whore? I began to feel an even stronger bond with Capt'n Peterson, but I would not commit suicide; so it would be off to the Philippines, or wherever that special base is. I could just see me sitting around with a bunch of GIs who were all dying and talking about how life isn't fair. I'd rather be in Vietnam flying than stuck in a medical compound waiting to die. I didn't say anything to anybody. This isn't fair! All I ever wanted to do was fly. I never did care about this stupid war!

CHAPTER 15

Damn War

A company of ARVNs and their American advisors, my bosses, began a sweep through the grassy sand dunes that were just inland from the beach and a little south of the Cau Viet River. This was the same area where Captain Peterson died. As was the normal outcome, they flushed out a Viet Cong. But this one took flight; I mean he was really hauling ass, running for his life. As we circled overhead, we could see the ARVNs shooting at him with their M16s and M79 grenade launchers; but he was just out of range for both. We could see the exploding rounds and the bullets kicking up the dust about twenty yards behind this potential Olympic sprinter. Gordy, our gunner, who occupied the M60 machine gun on the right side of the helicopter, received his orders; and so he pulled the trigger. *Ratta tat tat.* We watched the tracers head toward the enemy. The 7.62 machine gun rounds kicked up dust all around him, but none hit their target. Man, this guy could run! And carrying an AK47 rifle at that. Subconsciously, I started to root for him, unless he decided to use his rifle.

Come on, throw your gun down and give up, I thought to myself.

If he'd just throw down his rifle, we could land next to him, which would cause the ARVNs to stop firing; and we could take him prisoner. But he wouldn't drop his rifle. We couldn't land next to him unless he got rid of his rifle. He could open fire on us, and we couldn't take that chance. He was probably so scared that he didn't even realize that the rifle was still in his hand. Oh well, it was too late now. Our sprinter jumped into a ditch, no doubt exhausted. The ARVNs caught up with him in short order and killed him while he was lying there on the bank of the ditch.

We landed about twenty yards away from the dead VC. I knew that this was one sight that I really didn't need to permanently record in my brain; but for some morbid reason, I let Larry have the controls while I walked over to the ditch. The ARVNs and their American advisors were quite proud of their kill. One ARVN, wearing a big grin, who I assume was the victor, put his M16 up against the rectum of this obviously dead soldier and fired. *Thump*. Everyone thought that, that was funny. I laughed too. Coward, I thought to myself, why'd I laugh?

Now I know this was war, and we were there to kill or capture the bad guys before they came across the ocean and tried to kill my mother and father, who were now living in Denver. But after witnessing this event, which took less than half an hour, I came to realize something. This poor guy was probably a rice farmer with a small family and just wanted to be left alone. If the South Vietnamese government got to him first, he would be an ARVN; and if the North Vietnamese got to him first, then he would be part of the NVA. It didn't matter which government he lived under, he'd still be taxed. Tell me again, what were we there for? To free these poor people from what? I wouldn't dare share these feelings with anyone. My crew, the MACV bosses, and the ARVNs looked to me to perform a job; and they couldn't doubt my dedication for a second, nor would I let that happen.

I don't think I was the only one that had these feelings. It wasn't long after the runner lost his race that we got a call on the FM radio.

"Black Cat 30, this is Red One. We just had a prisoner escape, and we need some help."

This sounded exciting. We'd just left a small village about five miles southwest of his location and had a MACV major and his sergeant on board. I looked back and yelled that Red One needed help on the coast. Major Breen, who was a certified gung ho jerk and who didn't care for me and my crew because we weren't his idea of disciplined soldiers, nodded OK; let's go. Red One happened to be a Captain Petzold, who I didn't really know. He was fairly new in country, and we may have flown him only once or twice.

Larry, who had the controls, asked him for his location. Neither one of us recognized the name of the fishing village, so we just followed the FM needle that pointed at him every time he transmitted on the radio.

In just a few minutes, we saw Captain Petzold standing by his jeep parked in the sand next to some fishing boats that were pulled up on the sand about ten to fifteen yards from the surf. So Larry decided to land a few yards from the jeep, between it and the ocean, where the sand was damp and a little harder.

Captain Petzold looked surprised when he jumped into the helicopter and saw that his superior officer, Major Breen, was on board; and he wasn't smiling. He nodded in acknowledgement at

Major Breen and then turned to me and yelled, "He took off toward those trees," pointing toward an area about a quarter mile south and inland from the ocean. I think it was more for Major Breen's benefit than for me that he added, "He had plastic handcuffs on." I doubted that.

Larry, who still had the controls, nodded and took off over the ocean, into the wind, and then made an immediate right turn toward the trees. Within seconds, we came upon the area where the escapee was supposed to have taken refuge. The area was a mixture of trees and brush. It couldn't have been much more than a half mile across. We flew over the area at about one hundred feet but couldn't see anybody.

Captain Petzold yelled out, "Go ahead and open fire."

I didn't know what we were supposed to shoot at but figured that Cecil and Gordy needed the practice, so I told them to open fire. They were ready and started firing immediately.

After about ten minutes of our shooting trees, grass, and sand, Captain Petzold yelled, "Put 'er down over there, on the sand at the edge of the grove; and we'll look for him on foot."

I thought that, that was a dumb idea, but he was the boss. We were on short final when, as if to correct his dumb idea, he added, "Go to My Chanh and pick up some ARVNs who will be waiting for you and bring them back so we can sweep through the area." My Chanh was the name of an ARVN base where he was stationed.

OK, that's better, I thought, but said, "Yes, sir."

After Larry's landing, everyone jumped out of the helicopter except Major Breen. Leaning toward me, as if to make this battlefield order perfectly clear, he said, "This is my new lightweight backpack that I just got from the States. Drop it off at Hong Ha." That was his MACV outpost where he was stationed.

No please or thank you? I thought. "No problem, we'll drop it off," I said.

He paused as he looked me squarely in the eye, probably waiting for a "Yes, sir." Well, he wasn't going to get it from me.

He then exited the helicopter where an errant Captain Petzold was waiting, like a good little soldier, for his butt chewing, for losing his prisoner.

Since it was my turn to fly, I announced to Larry, "I've got the controls," and gently shook the cyclic as an indication that I had the controls. He gently shook the cyclic in return, indicating that it was all mine.

As we lifted off, I noticed that the low-fuel warning light was on, which comes on when there is only twenty minutes of fuel left.

"Larry, how long has that been on?" I asked, nodding toward the light.

"I don't know," he said, "this is the first time I've seen it."

Aw great! It would take a good twenty minutes to get to My Chanh, which was ten miles south of Quang Tri; get the ARVNs; and bring them back. Forget it, I thought. Major Jerk Face and his warriors were going to be on their own for a while. Yeah, I know, I've got this attitude problem. But it was also a good fifteen minutes back to Quang Tri Main for fuel. And we didn't even know how long the low-fuel warning light had been on. I got that sickening feeling in my stomach. The feeling that I've experienced so many times before. I didn't like it. I now had visions of a flameout and the subsequent autorotation to a rice paddy. I'd heard that to save fuel, you can beep the rotor RPM down from 100 percent to the bottom of the green. Probably wouldn't make any difference, but I had to try something. I'm too old for this. (Turned twenty a couple of months earlier.)

We made it to Quang Tri Main OK, which was a relief, like emptying a full bladder just in time.

Now it was on to My Chanh to pick up the ARVNs and then to the grove of trees to drop them off. The ARVNs were waiting for us as promised. After loading the eight soldiers, we headed for Captain Petzold and his troops. As we approached the grove of trees, Major Breen and party popped a blue smoke. Larry answered on the radio, "Roger, blue smoke."

I laughed at the thought of Captain Petzold receiving a fatherly lecture from Major Breen, all the time we were gone, which was a good half hour longer than what they expected.

I asked Larry, "Do you think they want us to come back and pick them up?"

"Don't know," he said.

After we landed, the ARVNs jumped out; but neither Major Breen nor Captain Petzold came over to the helicopter. Oh well, I thought, if they don't want to talk to us then they can figure out on their own how to get their butts home. So we departed the scene of the crime and headed toward Dong Ha, about seven miles northwest of Quang Tri, to drop off Major Breen's wonderful new state-of-the-art backpack.

As we approached the compound, I called on the radio to get someone to come outside the gate to the helicopter pad to pick up the backpack. But no one answered. I called again. No Answer. Hmmm.

I thought of landing on the pad, which was located just outside the main gate and on the opposite side of the road, then have Gordy run it into the commander's office. Na, too much work, I thought. So instead, I made the approach to an imaginary pad that I placed just above the thirty-foot tall flagpole which was located at the center of the compound. As we approached the imaginary plane,

I pulled the collective up a lot more than normal and stopped the Huey at a thirty-five-foot hover, just above the flagpole. I expected to see ARVNs scurrying out of their bunkers to see what was going on; and then maybe they would come over to the pad, and we'd give them the backpack. After all, the turbine engine, the whining tail rotor, and the *wop wop wop* of the main rotor blades were enough to wake the dead. But no one came out, and the main gate was wide-open. Now I don't have a great military mind; and admittedly, I had a bad attitude, but this didn't look right.

Still at a thirty-five-foot hover, over the intercom, I ordered, "Kick it out."

"What?" Cecil asked.

"Throw that damn backpack out," I ordered again.

You'd think I was ordering them to charge a machine gun nest. Or maybe worse, face Major Breen and explain what happened to his backpack.

"OK, bombs away," replied Gordy, as he kicked it out of the helicopter while holding on to the vertical brace that held his smoke grenades. *Ker plop*. It landed with a cloud of dust.

Remorse? Well, maybe for a second, then I was over it. Anyway, he *did* say, "Drop it off." And we complied with his exact orders. That actually felt kind of good.

That night, after supper and a feeble attempt to write a letter to my mom and dad, I went to the officers' club. Well, well, well, look who was there, Captain Petzold. Never seen him there before. Captain Petzold was a tall, stocky guy with blond hair who looked like he came from a rich family.

"I see you made it back OK." I politely started the conversation as I walked up to his table and sat down. I knew he was there to see me.

"Yes, we took the jeep back and left the ARVNs out there," he politely replied.

"Marc, you know that I am a 'marksman' with my .45," he said. After pausing, as if trying to find the right words, he continued, "I could have hit him. I mean, when he jumped out of the jeep, I pulled my .45 out; and . . . I could have easily shot him. But I didn't. I couldn't do it. I just couldn't bring myself to shoot him."

I couldn't believe it! He came to the bar to confess to me. But why me? Major Breen probably ordered him to come confess to me as his punishment. Or maybe his conscience was killing him. Either way, I guessed someone respected me.

Should I let him off the hook? Yeah, I let him off the hook. I began to say one thing while thinking something else.

"Aw, that's OK, Captain, we all probably have done something like that at some time in our life. Hell, I probably would have done the same thing."

"Really?" he asked.

"Sure," I replied.

"Thanks, Marc, this has really been bothering me."

"Don't worry about it," I said as I looked at the bartender and waved. He knew what I wanted.

Captain Petzold stood up from the table, where this confessional took place; thanked me again; and walked out. He didn't even order a drink. He was a strange one.

I sat there and nursed my scotch and water and wondered. Really, what would I have done? What's the difference between this guy that got away and the sprinter that was killed earlier? The sprinter possibly could have saved his life by throwing down his weapon and giving up. In that case, he lives. This other guy was already a POW and out of the war. He decided to get back in the war and subsequently might try to extend the war by killing my fellow Americans, my crew, or me. No choice there; I would have popped him.

I didn't like the conclusion I came up with. After all, I joined the army to fly and to get the one thousand hours of flying time so I could go back to Hobbs and fly for Dick Marshall. I really didn't like this war, or any war for that matter; but I put myself into the situation where I had no choice but play the game. I couldn't help but think of the hippie poster that said something like "What if there was a war and nobody came?" Too simplistic? Yeah, but a nice thought. Oh well, I joined the army so that I could fly; and that's what I was doing, and quite a bit too.

As for Captain Petzold, he never did find his prisoner. And I never saw him again, which suited me fine. He was no Captain Gene Peterson; that's for sure.

CHAPTER 16

The Sick, Wounded, and Dead

In supporting the ARVNs, we would often medivac their wounded soldiers, not to the American military hospitals, but to the ARVN hospitals. We noticed that when a South Vietnamese soldier was wounded, they seemed to go into shock easier than the American soldiers. We guessed that it was because the Americans knew that they had the best medical care in the world waiting for them, and maybe even a ticket home. The ARVN were already home, and the quality of their care was questionable.

This came to light when we were flying south from a firebase that was in the DMZ. Officially, it wasn't there; but we weren't in Cambodia or Laos either. We flew just over the top of a convoy of ARVN APCs (armored personnel carriers); when Cecil called out over the intercom, "Mr . . . . Mr . . . . Mr . . . . Williams," he finally blurted out, "One just blew up."

I knew what he meant; I flung the Huey around in a steep turn. As we completed the course reversal, we could see the smoke ascending from the visibly damaged APC. It was obvious that they were going to have casualties. While lowering the collective, I lined up my approach path for a landing in a grassy area about fifteen yards from the smoking APC. He'd hit a land mine. It didn't occur to me that there may be more there, and we could be landing on one; or our rotor wash could set one off. We didn't need it, but an ARVN popped a smoke for us. No one said a word as if this was a daily routine. As was the standard procedure any time we were picking up the dead or wounded, we didn't roll the throttle off but kept the rotor RPM at 100 percent, in case the cause for their being wounded or killed was still around. So as we gently touched down, the ARVNs from the other APCs had already pulled the first of the wounded out of the simmering APC and loaded them into our makeshift ambulance. One after another, they were placed in the seats and on the floor until there wasn't any more room. No stretchers, but none of our patients seemed to mind. "Could we take one more?" an ARVN asked Larry. "He has a hurt hand."

A young man with a bloody hand stood there, hoping that we would show him some mercy. Looking over the mass of suffering flesh, I saw a small space behind Larry's seat. I waved at the young soldier and pointed to the small space. As if in a race to get in before I changed my mind, he climbed over two of his comrades and curled up into the fetal position with his back to Larry's armored seat. Larry knew the routine and had the controls. He pulled pitch while I watched the torque gauge go 95 percent, then 100 percent, now 105 percent. I told Larry something he already knew, "We've got a load."

He responded, "Yeah."

While Larry pointed *Blivit* toward the ARVN hospital, I called ahead on the FM radio and told them that we have eleven on board, and our ETA (estimated time of arrival) was ten minutes. I then tried to describe the severity of their injuries. "Oh yes, one has a hand injury."

Larry called Quang Tri tower for clearance through their control zone, "Landing ARVN med." As Larry approached took him over the Constantia wire, Cecil and Gordon both looked back at the tail to make sure that we didn't stick the tail rotor into the coiled barbed wire, and in unison called out, "Tail clear."

The ARVN medical personnel and their American physician advisor ran up to the right side of the helicopter. They approached the helicopter bending over to make themselves a couple of feet shorter in order to avoid the spinning blades that were a good five feet above them. But those five feet could quickly be erased if either Larry or me accidentally kicked or pushed the cyclic to its stops. After they removed their patients, Larry called Quang Tri tower and advised them that we were leaving the ARVN med pad and requested clearance for landing at the POL for refueling. POL is the acronym for . . . well, I'm not sure; but that's where the very large fuel bladders were located. These bladders were kept out in the open, next to a small shack that contained the pumps. Our normal routine was to roll the throttle off but not shut down the engines. That was so that if a fire started or we started to receive mortar or rocket fire, we could immediately roll the throttle on, pull pitch, and get out of there. The fuel receptacle was a mere five feet from the hot exhaust of the engine. A spray of fuel that got ignited was a concern, so either Gordy or Cecil stood by the fire extinguisher. The aircraft commander or copilot were required to stay at the controls; so if the helicopter caught on fire, they could hover it away from the fuel bladders. I always wondered if we would do that rather than exit the oversized Molotov cocktail and hightail it out of there on a dead run.

We were just finishing refueling and were about to call the tower to get clearance for a south departure from the ramp to go back to the MACV citadel pad and call it quits for the day, when we got a call from dispatch.

"Black Cat 30, the navy needs your assistance five miles north of the Cau Viet. Seems that they can't get their launch back to their mother ship."

"Roger, on our way," I replied.

"This . . . this . . . this sounds interesting," Cecil responded over the intercom. "The . . . the navy needs our help!"

The location described was about a twenty-minute flight, and we now had two hours of fuel on board but only about an hour of daylight. Where we were going was no place to be and especially at night. We saw the navy frigate about a mile offshore; and as we proceeded northeast along the beach, we located the twenty-foot open launch sitting half in the water and half on the beach. It looked like an oversized flatbottom rowboat that was common, back in Kansas, only larger; and it had two large outboard motors attached to the stern. We landed next to the boat without the aid of colored smoke. I guess the two sailors didn't know the routine, but no matter. They were the only boat on the entire beach that stretched into North Vietnam.

After we touched down on the sand about twenty feet from the boat, we rolled the throttle off to idle. We were only a couple of miles from the DMZ and North Vietnam, and we didn't want to spend any more time here than necessary.

I pulled off my helmet and asked over the whine of the turbine engine, "What's the problem?"

I don't know if it was because he was embarrassed or just happy to see us, but the ensign, a big man with golden hair, had a big grin on his face. "We can't get the launch past the breakers."

"What do you want us to do?" I responded.

"Can you pull it out past the breakers into the open water?"

I looked at Cecil, who was standing next to the ensign. And without me having to say a thing, he already had a solution.

"We . . . we . . . we can wrap the rope that's tied to . . . to . . . to the bow of the boat around the machine gun brace then pull it through the . . . the . . . the cargo bay and tie it to the other gun brace."

I quite frankly didn't know how we were going to pull this off since helicopters aren't like trucks. While they're hovering, they are more like floating hot-air balloons, sensitive to outside forces like wind and waves. But Cecil has a degree in engineering; and what the hell, let's give it a shot.

Gordy stayed with his machine gun, which was facing North Vietnam so that in case they decided to charge across the line and attack us, he could single-handedly fight them off. Cecil took the lead in putting his idea to work, along with the two sailors as his assistants. He wrapped the rope around the left brace a few times and then tied it to the right gun brace. With everyone on board, I put my helmet on and rolled the throttle back on. I looked at Larry and smiled. We were two boys having a boatload of fun!

I slowly picked *Blivit* up to a high ten-foot hover and moved the Huey a few feet away from the boat to take the slack out of the rope. Then hovering backward, I dragged the boat in the sand, turning it around until the bow was facing the five-foot waves.

Oh my goodness, I thought, what if the boat sinks? We couldn't get the rope off the braces quick enough to free us; and as powerful as the Huey is, we couldn't lift a sinking armor-plated boat – especially when we were full of fuel. We'd go down with it! Oh well, it was too late now.

With the boat facing the incoming waves, we started to hover sideways. I watched the boat, looking for signs that this whole idea was insane. We remained at a steady ten- to fifteen-foot hover while the boat's bow shot up toward us as it hit each wave.

I could see why they couldn't get it past the waves, or why they didn't want to be in the boat while attempting. After about a dozen waves, we were in the smooth water. We continued to pull it toward the frigate when the ensign yelled, "This is good enough."

"Do you want us to drop you off in the boat?" I responded.

"No, they'll pick it up; just drop us off at Fifth Mec, in Quang Tri. The frigate will pick up the launch."

I'm glad he said that because once again, I'd volunteered to do something without thinking. Trying to drop someone off into a small boat would have been next to impossible and quite dangerous. The hurricane force rotor wash from the Huey would blow the launch away from us as we attempted to get close to it.

I nodded OK as if we could have pulled it off; and who knows, maybe we could have. Gordy untied the rope that was tied to his machine-gun brace, while Cecil carefully pulled it toward him, unwound it from his brace, and let it drop toward the crewless boat.

Yeah, I felt good about my crew and me that evening, just a couple of miles south of North Vietnam.

I gave the controls to Larry, and he pointed the helicopter toward Quang Tri. As he passed over the beach, he pulled the nose up a little so that he cleared a palm tree by a mere foot or two, and then over a series of sand dunes, rice paddies, and then on along the middle of the Qua Viet river until the aviation unit of the Fifth Mec was in sight. Larry's coming along nicely, I thought. He's a good pilot. He should be ready for his aircraft commander's check ride soon.

While Larry was taking his turn flying, I called the ARVN hospital on the FM radio to see how our APC victims, that we'd dropped off a few hours earlier, were faring. It turned out that the ARVN that was in the most serious condition was the one with the hand injury. He went into shock. Oh well, I'm glad we made room for him.

That night, everyone at our MAC V compound was talking about Black Cat 30. How we rescued the ARVNs and the navy. It turned out that an air force pilot, who was flying his observation aircraft in the area at the time, watched our rescue of the navy's boat. He came over to our compound to have a drink with us. That felt good! However, I was a little unnerved when we were told that after we left the APC with the injured ARVNs, they hooked up to the damaged APC to drag it out of the way; and after a few feet they hit another land mine.

"Crap, that's where we landed!" I let that slip out before I could catch it. Not allowing my next thought to escape too, I thought, I'm going to reach into my bag of tricks one of these times, and it's going to be empty!

"Give me another scotch." This was my superficial John Wayne answer to danger.

The next morning, dispatch told me that they needed our help over at the ARVN hospital. Leaving Larry at the controls after shutdown, Cecil and I started to walk toward the hospital when a nice-looking army captain in his late twenties, along with an older Vietnamese physician, came walking out to meet us.

With my, I-can-do-anything drawl, I asked, "How can we help you, sir?"

"We've got an ARVN in isolation with the plague; can you take him down to the MACV regional hospital in Hue? The medical facility there is much better equipped to help him."

I said, "Sure."

He interrupted me, "The plague is very, very contagious with little chance of cure."

Damn, did it again, volunteering my crew and me without thinking. Too late, my mouth was still running. "Maybe we can put some kind of isolation chamber in the helicopter and then fly him to Hue?"

He replied, "Thanks, let's see what we can come up with; I'll contact you tomorrow." He turned around and headed back to the hospital leaving the distinguished civilian doctor standing in front of me.

He looked at the departing captain, paused as if waiting to make sure that the American couldn't hear him and then spoke in actually quite-good English, "Sir, please do not do that. He will cause danger for you and your crew, anyway; he is going to die anyway." I was touched. He really cared about our welfare. "Come back tomorrow."

While most American soldiers referred to the Vietnamese with contempt and called them gooks, slant eyes, and so on; and I guess I did my share of it too. At that moment, I really regretted it.

Looking this man squarely in the eyes, I replied in the most sincere way I could, "Thank you sir, thank you very much."

He responded, "Tomorrow," then turned around and walked off.

That night in the MACV officers' club, I couldn't help but think, I did it again! Without thinking, I'd volunteered for a mission that could kill all of us. Maybe this would be the one that would bit me. But isn't that what war was all about? Taking chances and danger? Yeah, but the decisions that was put on this young man's shoulders were heavy. I had another scotch.

The next day, we fired up the helicopter and made the three-minute flight over to the ARVN hospital. The MACV doctor came out to the helicopter before we could shut it down and with a smile said, "Don't worry about the ARVN; he died last night."

"Dodged the bullet again," I thought as he continued.

"Gave him a blood transfusion with the wrong blood type; it killed him."

I thought to myself, Americans with incurable diseases get sent to the Philippines to die a slow death; ARVNs get it over with in a hurry and die overnight. That poor slob may be better off than I am, damn sluts.

"Thanks, sir, if there's anything we can ever do for you, let me know."

We regularly flew medivacs for the MACV and the ARVNs. And to show the world that we were wonderful people, the MACV had us fly injured civilians and those who were seriously sick  out to the hospital ships, the *Sanctuary* and *Repose*. These two ships took turns sailing between four to eight miles offshore between Hue and Quang Tri.

If the weather was bad, low clouds and visibility, then it could be quite difficult. They would have us in radar contact but weren't allowed to give us directions on finding them. They told us why once, but it sounded like a New York lawyer's explanation. However, since we were communicating with them on a FM radio from the time we were about to go feet wet (offshore), every time they transmitted, our FM radio's navigation needle would point in their direction. So we would call and ask questions about the wind, how far offshore they were, and how rough the sea was. All the while, the needle would point toward them.

This was especially beneficial on one such day when there was about a three-hundred-foot cloud base and half-mile visibility. While we were en route to take a very sick Vietnamese man to the *Repose*, we heard a marine Huey call in and ask for radar vectors. The navy controller advised him in the proper legalese that he couldn't help him with vectors. I jumped in and advised the marine pilot that if he tuned his directional finder to FM (like the car radio), it would point to the ship when the controller talked on the FM radio. Evidently, the marines didn't have the same equipment or he didn't understand, because after we dropped off our patient and started to head west back to shore, he was still trying to find the ship. Finally, in desperation (I could relate), he called us on the FM radio.

"Black Cat 30, I'm having some mechanical problems, and I'm going to land on the beach; could you meet me there and take my patient out to the *Repose?*"

"OK, no problem, we'll be there in about two minutes," I replied.

That's a big beach; how will I find him? I thought. Duh, the same way we find the ship; follow the needle.

"Marine helicopter, let us know when you land on the beach."

"OK, we've just landed," he replied, obviously relieved.

Got what we needed. The needle pointed just a little to the left of our nose. We adjusted our direction and continued. We spotted the breakers. Realizing that the beach was close now, we started to slow down. OK, I thought, there's the beach and there he is. We landed to his right, both facing the west. Cecil and Gordy got out and helped the marine crew move the patient over to our helicopter.

I'm not sure what his mechanical problem was; but before I could ask him if he needed help, his crew was back on board; he pulled pitch, radioed "thanks," and was off.

We turned around and started the short trek back to the *Repose.*

Finding the hospital ship was just part of the challenge of the mission. Landing on the back of a moving ship was quite challenging. Once we'd find the ship, the controller would give us the winds and swell. But unlike the land-based controllers, who would give the wind direction based on the compass rose (and the ground doesn't swell), the navy controller gives the wind direction relative to the nose of the ship. In addition, the ship was moving, so the wind speed was a combination of the outside airspeed and the speed of the ship. What does that have to do with anything? Well, we had to basically chase the ship, while landing into the wind. That means, depending on the normal winds, we could be landing on the ship while flying twenty or thirty knots per hour. Add to that, the ship was going up and down in the waves, which caused the helicopter pad, which was located on the rear deck of the ship, to swell or go up and down. When the ocean is rough, this could be over twenty feet. So after making a fast approach, we ended up over a small deck that was going up and down. The trick was to slowly lower the collective until the skids (in a Huey it's the rear part of the skids) touched the pad. Once this happens, you must lower the collective rapidly in order to stay  on the pad. If you lower the collective too slowly, the pad will go down without the helicopter and then meet the helicopter which is on its way down when the pad is on its way up. This results in a very hard collision, which causes the helicopter to catapult off the pad like a trampoline. This is very dangerous and often fatal.

Over the months, I had quite a bit of experience landing on the hospital ships, perhaps more than anyone else currently flying in Vietnam. Needless to say, I was very confident.

So when Colonel Owens asked me to take him and some other officers out to the *Repose* at night, I didn't hesitate to accept the mission, thinking that it couldn't be that much different than in the day.

Well, it was a cloudy, windy night, and the ship was about six miles offshore. Just about the time we got to the ocean, we could see the boat. It was lit up like a Christmas tree from bow to stern. As we set up for an approach, we noticed that there wasn't a horizon. We needed to see a horizon to fly. No problem, I thought, as long as we got the *Repose* in sight, it will be our horizon. Then when we depart to go back to Quang Tri, we can use the flight instruments until we see the few lights of Quang Tri.

We were now on approach coming in from the right rear section of the boat. The winds were a relative forty knots, and the swell was twenty feet. Uh oh, I thought to myself. This isn't good. I didn't express my concerns with the crew because I didn't want them to be worried. I'd worry enough for all of us.

I could now see the navy signalman who had lights up in each leg, his body, and on his arms and paddles. That looked cool. As I slowly hovered over the pad, he continued to signal us closer, to get us over the center of the pad. As we hovered over the pad, waiting for the right moment to start lowering the collective in order to touch the pad, it hit me – vertigo.

The ship was rocking back and forth, but there was no natural horizon to rationalize it in my brain. It appeared like the Earth's horizon was rocking back and forth. Bad vertigo! I was having trouble hovering over the pad and was starting to creep toward the hull of the ship, just a few yards to my right. The signalman now started a new maneuver that I didn't have any trouble recognizing, the wave-off. But if I took off now, with vertigo and instantly seeing nothing but black, we would crash. I was sure of that. So I took a chance and lowered the collective, hard. Luck would have it; we just caught the pad as it was going down. It wasn't smooth, but we were alive. Everybody got out as if nothing out of the ordinary happened. I didn't say anything to anybody, but I knew that we were almost a statistic.

CHAPTER 17

A Direct Order

I'd been in country for about eight months now, and the monsoons had set in. The timing of the monsoons north of the Hai Van Pass was just the opposite of that to the south. Plus our monsoons were cold, at least compared to those of the south. The constant rain, fog, and mist were depressing and stressful to fly in. Plus we couldn't go to the beach. We were cold and it seemed that every civilian male in Vietnam has a U.S. issued flight jacket; but nooooo, we couldn't get one. Fortunately, Charlie didn't like this weather either, and wasn't that active. Or maybe we just chose to ignore him.

Larry has been gone for a while. He took his aircraft commander's

Ron White's on the left

check ride and passed. He's flying out of Da Nang now. So my new copilot was Ron White. Ron was a nice kid, imagine that; I'm not the youngest pilot anymore so I get to call the new pilots "kid."

The rainy days were long and boring, sitting in the helicopter with all the doors shut, writing letters, or sleeping. We were all tired of talking.

It was during one of those endless days that we heard that the generals down at Phu Bi were going to give Colonel Owens a going-away party since he was about to rotate back to the States. Hue was about forty-five miles to the south of Quang Tri, and Phu Bi was another five miles south of Hue. Normally, we'd jump at the chance to fly and especially where the food was very good, as it was at the MACV Hdq. base in Phu Bi. The problem was that the weather was terrible – fog, drizzle, and very low visibility. We would have to fly down Highway 1 by Camp Eagle, the home of the 101st Airborne, then past Hue's citadel with its radio towers, then on to the MACV in Phu Bi. This was clearly too dangerous and frankly; I wasn't that familiar with the area around Hue. I knew my limits and felt that this mission was beyond my ability to accomplish it safely.

So I told Cecil and Gordy to unfasten the panels; and then I'd tell Colonel Owens that we're doing a twenty-five-hour inspection, and we couldn't fly. I didn't care anything about pulling a twenty-five-hour inspection, but it was a good excuse to keep us on the ground. Sure enough, up drove Colonel Owens along with his gopher boy, Lieutenant Jenks, and Colonel Owens's new replacement, Colonel Santa Cruz, who I hadn't met yet.

"Need to go to Phu Bi," barked Colonel Owens.

"Can't, sir, we're doing a twenty-five-hour inspection." For the first time since I got my warrant officer's bar and wings, an officer locked my heels. While standing at attention in the cold drizzle, he chewed me up one side and down the other for not having the inspection done earlier.

"Sir," I responded, "the only way we can go is if you declare this a tactical emergency." That was my trump card and he knew it.

"I'm declaring this a tactical emergency," he snarled with gritted teeth.

Oh crap, I thought, now we have to go. This was the same as a direct order in combat, the type of order where they could shoot you for disobeying or send you to prison for a long, long time. Either way, I didn't care. After all, my urine was now even more contaminated with puss than ever, and I wasn't going home.

"Cecil, button 'er up," I called out. It only took a minute to snap everything back in place.

Now there's one thing helicopters didn't do in Vietnam, at least in these parts; and that was fly IFR, in the clouds, the soup. The clouds were full of F-4 jets, C-130 transports, and turbo prop (fixed-wing) aircraft, but *no* helicopters. Slow-moving helicopters we're not welcomed in their club. Plus the air traffic controllers wouldn't give us the time of day. So off we went heading south, following Highway 1. The windshield wipers were slapping at the rain on the windshield, but they didn't help much.

I got that sinking pain in my stomach, the feeling that I learned to loathe. "This stinks," I said over the intercom. If we continued and went IFR in the clouds, I'm not sure what our way out would be, let alone two ways out. I could normally visualize us completing a mission, but this time I couldn't and I couldn't just hope that we make it.

After five to ten minutes of straining to see the road ahead of us, plenty of time to make sure that the weather wasn't just a local phenomenon, I told Ron over the intercom, "Take us back;

I'm not going to kill us all just so he can go to a party!" I turned around and yelled out in the direction of our passengers, careful not to look Colonel Owens in the eyes. "The weather's too bad; we're going back."

Colonel Owens didn't say a word. When we landed, I expected to get another butt chewing and maybe the assurance that I was in trouble. I guess he just gave up on me because no sooner did the skids touch, he jumped out of the Huey and stormed off with his entourage trailing behind him. I announced over the intercom, "I guess I disobeyed a direct order. Tactical emergency? I didn't give a rat's ass about that. It wasn't an emergency, and I wasn't going to risk our lives for a party."

I guess I expected a "Yeah, and he farts too," but there wasn't a response. It didn't matter; I knew I made the right decision.

I've been in Vietnam for almost nine months, and I was tired. I was tired of the stress. I was tired of the feeling of dread and doom, the feeling that at any moment we could be shot down. I was tired of wondering, when I wake up in the morning if this is going to be the day I die. I was tired of the close calls. My youthful eight-year-old's grin has been gone for a long time. My emotions were shot. They've been stressed to the limit; and my crutch, my drinking, has been out of hand for a long time. My urine was still full of puss. In fact, it's been getting worse. I was tired of feeling that I'm not going home and that I've got what Gene had. But shouldn't there be other symptoms? I mean if I have an incurable venereal disease, shouldn't it burn when I pee? Or shouldn't I be getting sick or something? There's just the puss, lots of puss. I wish Gene would have opened up to me and told me about what he was going through. I'd really like to know what his symptoms were. I was tired. I didn't even feel like going to the club and having a drink.

CHAPTER 18

Back to Da Nang

It was now the end of April, and I had about three months to go. Ha! Go where? As was the routine for the last eight months, Every week or so, we'd take our helicopter back to Marble Mountain to have routine maintenance performed. It was during one of these overnight maintenance trips that my commanding officer, Major Moore, called me into his office. This almost always meant that you're in trouble. What'd I do wrong? Oh well, what's he going to do? Cut my hair and send me . . .

"Mr. Williams," he said, "I just got a letter of recommendation from a Colonel Santa Cruz." Colonel Owen's replacement who was with him on the day that we were to take them to Hue for the going-home party. "This is the best letter of recommendation I've ever seen." He then proceeded to read it to me. It said something about my ability to "make critical decisions . . . weighing the mission against the danger of the loss of life . . ." and so on.

I guess it was impressive, but I really didn't care so I didn't pay a lot of attention to what he was reading. After all, I wasn't going home. Put it on my tombstone, I thought to myself.

"Mr. Williams, would you like to be a cat doctor?" Major Moore asked.

A cat doctor? That was the call sign for the maintenance test and recovery pilots, a very prestigious position. Only the very best are chosen to be cat doctors. Since I had my fill of Quang Tri and really needed a change, I replied, "Yes, sir, I can do it." So it was one more week in Quang Tri and then back to Marble Mountain with my meager belongings and my quite-active puss factory.

There were two cat doctors, Frank Loebs, my new roommate, and me. As cat doctors, we would test-fly the aircraft before and after the maintenance crew worked on them and when a company helicopter went down, either shot down or with mechanical problems. We would take turns going out with a special crew and try to recover the ship. This was a nice change from flying out in the wild, since now most of my flights would be around Marble Mountain Airfield, that is, unless we went out to recover a downed aircraft.

I really enjoyed learning about the workings of the Huey. My confidence increased daily as I listened to the mechanics as to why she reacted the way she did. I didn't find test flying the Huey to be stressful at all. I knew what I was looking for and how to find it. I needed this training to finish me off as a professional pilot.

It was about this time that I received a letter from Paula. As mentioned before, I'm a terrible letter writer, and I received numerous complaints from my parents, Paula, and Pat that I didn't write enough. So what few letters I wrote consisted mainly of "How are you? I am fine. The food is good and I'm safe." What else could I say? "Almost died today . . . oh yes, there's still puss in my urine."

I felt bad about not writing, but I didn't know what to do. Although I should have seen it coming, Paula's letter was quite a surprise to me. I guess I got the infamous "Dear John" letter. She said that she met a sailor and blah, blah, blah; and they got married. She deserved someone better than me and I knew it, but a sailor? The pain that I felt wasn't so much that she found someone else, as much as it was for leading her on for so long. I mean I was dating other girls and talking marriage while I was engaged to Paula. What a jerk. What is wrong with me? I don't have a moral fiber in my body. But it wasn't that I didn't want to marry *her*, it was just that I didn't want to get married period. That doesn't make sense, does it? Anyway, I should have treated her better. I started to recall the times we spent together and wondered if maybe she was the one. Oh well, it's too late now.

"Well, I still have Pat." Man! what a jerk I am!.

As in most modern wars, finding parts for the war machines was critical. For the 282nd Maintenance Platoon, it was no different. And like all those mechanics who came before us, we had to be ingenious in finding those parts that we couldn't get through normal channels. Our black market parts supply was located on the opposite side of Marble Mountain Airfield. It was the few, the proud, and the brave, the marines, or jarheads as we called them; and they flew the same type of helicopters. Fortunately for us, the marine's enlisted men were not allowed alcohol, other than the watered-down 3.2 percent beer. A fifth of whisky, which flowed like water on the army side, would get you just about anything you wanted from these guys.

So it was on a hot afternoon in June, our maintenance sergeant, who was our expert negotiator, and I embarked on one of these black market runs. We were in need of a hydraulic servo. I normally didn't go on these outings, but I was bored with just sitting in the hangar. We carefully placed several bottles of whiskey on the back floorboard of the jeep, covered them with a blanket, and commenced to drive over to the marine side.

We pulled up in front of the marine helicopter maintenance shed, which sat just off the aircraft ramp. As we climbed out of the jeep, we heard a loud *CLACK, CLACK, CLACK*. Although I'd never heard that sound before, I knew instantly what it was. I looked up, and I saw all four blades leaving the two marine Cobras, all in different directions. What took place now would be permanently burned into my mind. The two Cobras were flying in formation about four hundred feet above the runway and about a half block in front of us. They were about to begin a maneuver called a high overhead. This is a descending turn to the right that would end up with them being over the same spot on the runway but at a hover. They would then hover over to the adjacent parking ramp just in front of us. Something had gone terribly wrong. I watched in horror as both aircraft rolled over on their backs in slow motion. Everything was intact except they were missing their rotor blades. The four pilots (two in each aircraft) became my bothers; although I didn't know them, they were fellow helicopter pilots, and they were about to die. As they were trained, they immediately went into their crash positions: they pulled their feet back, knees up, then bent over and put their heads between their knees, and then put their hands over the backs of their necks to keep their heads down. The five seconds that it took to fall from four hundred feet until impact took five minutes. Then *WHOMP!* They hit the runway.

That's strange, I thought, there's no explosion. Maybe they'll live? Then the fuel, rockets, and munitions all ignited in both aircraft at the same time with a tremendous explosion. They were dead. Just ten seconds earlier, they were alive, maybe joking with each other, or most likely showing off. Now they were dead. As I watched the crash crews spray foam on the wreckage, I thought, four families back home will be receiving notices tomorrow. I could visualize their families when the chaplain knocks on their door. The emotional breakdowns and the broken hearts that will never heal. Damn!

Flying is so unforgivable. How do you get such a vivid image out of your mind? That very well could have been me! God knows how many close calls I've had with other aircraft. Normally, it would be another night of getting drunk in our little officers' club in Quang Tri. I guess that's how I coped. But that night, I was to be back in the aircraft commander's seat testing an aircraft that would be needed for a mission the next morning.

I didn't have the luxury of saying, "I don't want to fly anymore; it's too dangerous!" We were at war, and things like that happened. The lessons of that day would never be forgotten. Momentary distractions can cause a midair collision, and a midair collision can kill a good pilot. I was as good as they come; and if distracted at the wrong time, I would die too.

CHAPTER 19

Day of Reckoning

It had now been about a month since my move back to Marble Mountain, and I was scheduled to go home in fifty-seven days, when I got word that I was to report to the flight surgeon for my annual flight physical. I've been dreading this day for a long time, judgment day. As I sat in the examination room, the events of the previous ten months went through my mind, especially thoughts of Captain Peterson. Yeah, I couldn't help but notice that my urine specimen that I provided the male nurse was full of puss.

The doctor entered into the examination room where I sat on a metal chair next to the counter that held the neat tools that I was playing with a minute earlier.

"Mr. Williams," the flight surgeon paused.

"Oh crap, here we go," I muttered under my breath as I started to cringe, bracing myself for that same message that Gene must have received from Major Fitzpatrick.

"You've got one nasty bladder infection."

"Bladder infection?" I asked in disbelief.

"That's right."

"Will I be able to go home?"

"Yes, of course."

This fine-looking man, and smart too, just took a load off my shoulders that was bigger then the war itself! He brought me back from the dead! "Thank you, sir, yes, sir; I'll take the medicine, sir; may I go now, sir?" I didn't want him to change his mind or stop and think that maybe he'd better take a closer look at this guy's pee. For the first time since I got off that DC-8 stretch, I felt that I was going to make it out of this war alive. I couldn't help but think of the waste of good worry and stress because I didn't want to have my urinary tract infection checked out. Maybe there really wasn't an incurable bladder disease. Maybe Gene really didn't . . . No, I just dodged another bullet.

Now if I could just keep from volunteering for stupid missions, I'd be OK.

"Hey, Marc, I'm going to take some navy spotters up to direct their big guns on a NVA stronghold just south of here. Do you want to go? I need a copilot."

"Sure, let's go," I replied. What? Did I just volunteer to go out there where there's a war? Crap, I am a coward! No, not because of the fear of being killed, but because I didn't want to disappoint Daren. Once again, the fear of displeasing man, or rather the inordinate desire to please man, had got me in trouble. I've got to get over this hang-up, or it will kill me. In fact, it's a wonder I haven't already died. Come on, it's not that bad; it's probably normal anyway. Oh brother! Add to my list of screwed up phobias that I've started to talk to myself and out loud too. That's hard to explain to those who overhear me.

We picked up the two navy spotters, their radio gear, and headed south from Marble Mountain. We passed the two marble columns that stick up several hundred feet above the beach and then went feet wet. After about fifteen minutes, we started to climb up to the assigned altitude of three thousand feet and then moved inland to the area where the NVA was supposed to have a stronghold. I could see the battleships offshore and wondered about the huge shells that they were about to lob at the spot just below. How close were they going to be to us? Even though I made a D in geometry, it looked like those shells would have to come awfully close to us. I didn't say anything. I just assumed that the navy guys knew what they were doing. Up above us, a platoon of our company gunships circled, loaded for bear. I didn't realize it at the time, but this was a major operation. At this point, my memory gets hazy, and then it is completely wiped clean. The spotters directed the battleship's fire as we circled above, but I don't remember the explosions. They must have been huge. When they stopped, that was the signal that the army's armored unit was to move in – the tanks and armored personnel carriers. But I don't remember that either. I can only remember that we went down for a closer look, down to about a fifty feet. We flew by a hut, and there was an old man standing out in front. He must have been standing there to let us know that he was of no danger to us. I was hoping that our right gunner wouldn't open fire and kill him. Our company gunships that were still circling overhead called us on the radio, "Black Cat (can't remember the call sign), get out of there; we're going to sweep the area."

I echoed their request over our intercom. "Darin, we have no business being down here; let's get out of here."

Thankfully, he complied with my request. I really didn't want to come unglued but was ready to do so. We were in a serious battle.

Later I was told that scores of NVA were flushed out of their hiding place and that our gunships swooped down for the kill. The NVA was trapped by the river, which I was told ran red with their blood. After the assault began, we headed home.

I got another air medal with a *V* (for valor) for that one.

CHAPTER 20

Emptiness

S ince I found out that I wasn't going to infect all the ladies of Australia with a dreadful venereal disease and my bladder infection wasn't infectious, I decided that I'd go to Sydney, Australia, for some much-needed R&R (rest and recuperation). Maybe that will help me get over whatever it is that's causing me to lose my eight-year-old's grin.

I spent seven days partying, sightseeing, and meeting some awful nice people. I did all the things that was suppose to make an all-American boy happy. But what I found was that the trip . . . well, it made me feel empty.

I knew that I was missing something, but I didn't know what. Maybe I was just ready to go home and see my parents. Maybe I'm ready to get married after all and have a family. Imagine me a dad? You don't suppose that Paula's Dear John letter hurt me more than I thought. Perhaps I need to start going to church . . . Na, I didn't like religion, although I was raised a Presbyterian. I went to one or two services that were held at the Marble Mountain Chapel, but I didn't get anything out of it. In fact, I felt that the clergy were there to soothe our conscience so that we could do things that were against our conscience. Then there was our maintenance copilot. He didn't have his aircraft commander's orders and had no experience outside of the local area, so he had to fly with Frank or me. He was a nice kid and all, maybe a little too righteous for me. We would sit in the helicopter and talk while the mechanics worked on whatever it was that we found that was amiss. I don't know what religion he has. I didn't ask and didn't care. But he told me things that Presbyterians never talked about, the Bible book of Revelation. He'd tell me about the strange seven-headed wild beast coming out of the sea, and there would be a war so bad that blood would be up to the bridle of a horse, and so on. I have to admit that I found this quite interesting. But that didn't last long. I was curious that there may be something to what he was saying, so two different times I asked him to show me in his Bible where it said these things. He couldn't. So much for that.

I was flying days again, so I needed something to do with my nights. I had trouble falling asleep, but I was tired of getting soused at the club. I wanted some association so I decided to join some friends in playing cards, poker. No-limit poker. These guys were serious. One gunship pilot would put his .38-caliber pistol on the table, signifying that nobody better try and cheat. Come on, give me a break! We're officers (warrant) and gentlemen, and there's not much of a chance that we're going to cheat. He didn't scare me, but maybe he should have. He had pictures of dismembered enemy soldiers on his wall. He needed help.

My dad was reported to be quite a gambler; at least that's what I heard. Judging from our standard of living, he must not have been too good. But like a good father, he thought that I should know how to play cards so that others wouldn't take advantage of me.

My friends didn't take advantage of me. I actually did quite well. Most nights I'd win; and those nights that I didn't, I'd break even. It was fun, and by the time I got back to my hutch, I was exhausted and had no trouble falling asleep. It was the successful end of another day, mission accomplished. But when I'd wake up, I felt guilty for taking my friends' money. Where did this conscience thing come from?

The days clicked off ever so slowly. I had the game won. Now it was just a matter of running out the clock. I didn't volunteer for any more missions.

We now had a new company commander, who was nice enough, but I tried to avoid him as much as possible. With my experience and seniority, he could assign me to the type of missions or assignments where I'd be lined to get a medal; and I don't need any more medals. So I was expecting the worse when he called me into his office.

"Mr. Williams, we would like you back here at the 282nd and if you'll extend your tour for six months, we'll let you do whatever you want. Would you like to go back up to Quang Tri?"

I was actually tempted. I missed flying out of Quang Tri, and I missed Cecil, Gordy, and Larry. We were a team, a good team. I even missed *Blivit*. It wasn't the same flying out of Marble Mountain. I did like being a senior pilot, and I was just promoted to chief warrant officer (CW2). *What was I thinking?* With all the close calls that I'd had and the near-death experiences, one of these times the chips are going to fall on the other side of the statistical line.

Acting as if saying no was a real disappointment; I answered, "Sir, I'd rather fly with the 282 than with anybody else, but no, thanks."

But what really worried me was that I actually wanted to say yes. I wanted to please him. But I said no. Maybe there is hope for me.

Now, my main ambition in life was to just do my job and not volunteer for any missions.

Unfortunately, under the job description for my title, "recovery pilot," was "attempt to recover downed company aircraft." One such aircraft was just shot down about twenty miles southwest of Da Nang, and it was my turn to go after it. This should be a fairly routine mission, but the new company commander wanted to play too. Aw crap, I thought, it's medal time.

The game plan was that he would circle the crash site in another Huey at about two thousand feet above the ground and let me know if there were any bad guys around and which way the wind was blowing. Then if something went wrong and we went down, he would come to our aid. This was fine with me because that meant that he'd be way above us and out of the way.

Our company commander got over the downed aircraft first and gave us the wind direction and speed, easterly at about ten knots. OK, this will work. I decided to fly low level in a westerly direction about a quarter mile north of the wounded aircraft. I hoped that Charlie would think that we were going to the firebase that was about five miles farther west. When we were adjacent to the downed aircraft, we'd make a sharp left turn and dart over to the crippled Huey and land just west of it. Without shutting down, we would drop off the recovery crew and take off. They were good and had done this trick numerous times before. A Chinook, a large twin-rotor helicopter, would then swoop down, hook up to the bird, and up, up, and away; it'd be out of here. I would then come back and pick up the recovery crew. All this before the bad guys even knew we there or at least could get to us.

Everything was going as planned. Upon passing the aircraft off to our left, I began a steep left turn. As I rolled out of the turn, I was lined up on a spot just this side of the downed aircraft. But we had a problem. We had a tailwind. The winds were actually out of the west. I should have verified their wind report. I was already coming in a little too hot, but now we were approaching our LZ much too fast, plus we were heavily loaded. This is the formula for a dangerous condition called settling with power. (Simply put, the opposite of what is normal, the more power that is applied, the more lift that is lost until you hit the ground very hard.) We're committed. I didn't want to overfly the downed aircraft and make a teardrop loop, come back, and approach from the other direction. I flared the Huey hard, raising the nose way above the horizon, and pulled pitch. I allowed the aircraft to gain a little altitude because I didn't want to stick the tail rotor in the trees. I immediately reduced the flare and lowered the collective, reducing power. Then not as radical as before, I raised the nose again and pulled pitch. Then I allowed the nose to come back down and slightly lowered the collective. Then one more slight flare and little more collective. Touchdown. The back of our skids touched first; and then like a rocking chair, our well-behaved bird rocked forward until we were firmly planted on the ground. But this was all for naught. As soon as we touched down, a mortar exploded just behind us. So much for sneaking in. The recovery crew knew what the explosion meant. They weren't going anywhere. I immediately pulled pitch and took off, downwind. Power, I needed more power, 110 percent on the torque gauge. That's more than were allowed to pull. At this point I didn't care if I overtorqued the drivetrain. With the skids slicing through the top of the trees, we now held 105 percent until we went through translational lift. We stayed just above the trees until the airspeed indicator indicated 85 knots and then I pulled back on the cyclic made and started a rapid climb to 1,500 feet. Then it was back to Marble Mountain.

It turned out that Charlie was on a ridgeline just to the south of the downed aircraft and could see everything that was going on. He could have destroyed the downed helicopter anytime he wanted but was using it as bait. It was a trap meant for my crew and me.

CHAPTER 21

Homeward Bound

The last few days before I was to go home, I started to feel disenfranchised from my unit and friends. It was as if they didn't want to invest any more time and emotions on a relationship that was going to be gone in just a few days. Or maybe it was because I took all their money in the final poker game. Yeah, I was ready to go home. That day finally arrived on July 8, 1970. There was no going-home party for me. I don't remember anyone else getting one either. It was just the rotation; new ones would replace those leaving. It was as if the year I spent in Vietnam didn't really matter. What a shame.

I flew down to Cam Ranh Bay on an Air Force ferry flight and then boarded a DC-8 stretch for my trip back home. I was full of mixed emotions. Yes, I was going home, but I couldn't help but think of my friends that I left behind, the events of the last year, and Captain Gene Peterson. Should I go by and see his family? What would I tell them? The truth? No, guess I'd better leave that one alone.

After landing in Oakland, I boarded a United flight to Denver. My folks met me at the airport. It was so good to see them. I remember standing there with my mom and dad. After the hugs, tears, and more hugs, I looked around and couldn't help but notice that no one cared about my coming home. No one cared about what I went through just days before, and no one cared about Captain Peterson. I'm not sure what I wanted. Maybe if they knew what young men and women were going through, they would . . . what? I guess it's just part of the rotation.

After staying with my parents for about a week, I told them that I needed to go Atlanta to pick up the new Chevy Camero that I ordered a couple of months ago. I guess I went a little crazy once I found out that I could actually go home. I know my parents were disappointed, but I was really antsy. I needed to keep moving and didn't know what I wanted. My dad understood, but I'm not so sure my mom did.

I called Pat and she agreed to meet me in Atlanta at the airport. We would pick the car up at the dealer, and then I'd drive her back home to Cocoa Beach, Florida. Here we go again. Was I now ready to get married? I actually hoped so.

Pat met me at my gate, and my, my, my, she looked great. A real southern belle. We got my bags and took a cab to the Chevy dealer. There it was, a 1970 Chevrolet Camero. It was dark blue with a white interior, 307 V-8, three-speed transmission and an AM/FM radio. This car was really nice, and it was all mine. Paid in full. We drove back to Cocoa Beach where I spent a couple of days with Pat and her parents, and then I drove my new car up to my new assignment at Fort Stewart, Georgia. This was the exact same place where I finished my flight training just a little more than a year earlier.

But it was different. The place was full of flight instructors who had spent the same length of time in Vietnam, flying Hueys just like me. Oh, they may have flown different missions, some more dangerous and some not. My wonderful flying skills and my keen senses needed for making life-and-death decisions weren't appreciated or needed here. I was made the company safety officer and processed the flight records of the flight students, now mainly Vietnamese. To say that my heart wasn't in it would be a ghastly understatement. My workweek was just three and a half days long. So I spent most of my time either at Pats, in Cocoa Beach, or hanging out with my roommate, Allen Sodergren, who I went to flight school with, and some of the guys I flew with back at the 282ⁿᵈ.

Now I didn't smoke weed while I was in Nam. I wouldn't even consider it. Drinking and smoking cigarettes were bad enough. Anyway, the Army blessed the abuse of alcohol and provided cigarettes free in our C-rations and for only $1.75 a carton for those of us who chain-smoked. But using drugs was not tolerated. I wasn't introduced to the world of drugs until after I arrived back in Savannah, and then by other pilots who did partake while they were in Vietnam.

I did get checked out in a new OH-13, not unlike the ones I learned how to fly in back in Fort Walters. Yes, I still had the love of flight. But I didn't get to fly much at all. I was bored. I wanted to fly. My job was boring, and being a safety officer was a joke. I developed a really bad attitude. In fact, one day our company commander called Allen and me into his office and shared with us the brilliant metaphor, "You can't pound sand up a dead mule's ass." Allen and I just looked at each other. We weren't quite sure if we were the mule, the ass, the sand, or the pounder.

Then opportunity knocked. The army announced that they had too many warrant officers and offered an early-out program for those who had already had a tour of duty in Vietnam. I was second in line. (I would have been first, but I was sitting in the back of the room when the announcement was made and couldn't get to the front any faster.)

So after just under three years of a four-year obligation, I got out of the army. In just a couple of days, I would be leaving Fort Stewart, Georgia, and the U.S. Army for good. Well almost, as a warrant officer I would continue to be in the in-active reserves. This meant that I could be called back at any time. That's OK; I could live with that.

But before I could get out, I had to go by all of the different services and get a signature from each department showing that there was no unfinished business that would keep me in the army. This included an exit physical. Should I tell them that I still had the bladder infection that I contracted about a year earlier in Quang Tri? And should I tell them that my hearing was now shot because of the turbine engines? *Hell no!* I didn't want to take any chances that they might say that I couldn't get out because they needed to treat me first. So mum was the word. Anyway, on my flight physical that I took about a month prior, I put down in the remarks section that I still had a bladder infection. Of course, no one ever reads the notes.

CHAPTER 22

A New Life

Finally, I was free and it felt good. I loaded all my worldly positions, which didn't amount to much more than my stereo, some civilian clothes, and my puss machine, in my Camero, and headed south to Cocoa Beach to see Pat. I told her that I was going to Colorado and that after I got there, I'd send for her. Then it was off to Denver where my parents were eagerly awaiting my arrival.

Why Denver, when there was a nice job flying helicopters offshore in the Gulf of Mexico? To entice me to come to Denver, my dad had told me that he knew the VP of United Airlines and that there was a job flying for United waiting for me when I got there. YES! I could see me as an airline pilot! (Girls like airline pilots!) I arrived the day before Christmas, 1970. I must say that it was nice to be back home, but this time it was without a uniform and all the uncertainties that came with that.

After a few weeks, it became evident that my dad was overly optimistic. There wasn't an airline pilot's job waiting for me. In fact, they were laying off pilots. Oh well, I didn't get upset. After all, Mom and Dad just wanted me home, even if only for a little while.

I stayed in Colorado, for about three months, collecting unemployment and smoking weed with my cousin Pam. However, I did one positive thing while being there. I went to Fitzsimmons Army Hospital and received treatment for my bladder infection. After about three months of treatment, it finally went away, no more puss. I guess I should have celebrated. After all, a very bad chapter of my life was finally closed. Well, not really. Now I had to live with the damage that the infection had caused. And oops, I forgot to send for Pat, or even call her. Oh well, she was probably so mad at me by that time that she wouldn't talk to me anyway.

I called Dick Marshall back in Hobbs, New Mexico, to see if I could fly for him. He said come on down, and we'll talk about it. So off to Hobbs I went in my new Chevy Camero. Hobbs was where I graduated from high school and started my flying career. And it's where I had the brilliant idea of joining the army.

After Dick saw that I still had all my body parts and had no evidence of visible damage, he offered me a job flying charters and flight instructing. In fact, he had been telling everybody, "Remember Marc the gas boy? He's coming back from Vietnam, and he's going to fly for us."

That was nice. His attitude was much different now than the day he told me that I couldn't fly commercially for him until I had one thousand hours of flying time. Now with over one thousand hours of flight time, I met that insurance requirement. So back to Denver I went to pack my belongings and say goodbye to my parents. This time, it was a little different since I wasn't going to war.

I moved into a cheap apartment and reported to Dick for work. He immediately sent me on a short flight to Midland, Texas, but there really wasn't a whole lot more for me to do since I didn't have a FAA flight instructor's rating. I decided to go to Meacham Field, in Fort Worth, Texas, where I attended a flight school called Acme School of Aeronautics. Acme specialized in quick cram courses. For ten days, I flew and studied until I was ready to take my flight instructor's check ride with the FAA. It wasn't all cram and fly though. While I was there, I dated a pretty blonde Texas girl who worked at Acme as a secretary. Her name was Linda Sue. So after finishing my training, I said goodbye to Linda Sue and went back to Hobbs. The following week, I went to the FAA District Office in Lubbock, Texas, where I was to take my check ride.

The flight instructor rating is the hardest FAA rating to obtain. I was told that my examiner, Frank Robinson, liked to flunk you the first time around just to show you who's boss. That's OK with me. I've been taking military check rides for over two years, and I learned how to do it. It's all in your mind. I'd pretend that I was flying a mission in Vietnam or flying a charter. I'm the aircraft commander (or civilian = "pilot in command"), and I know what I'm doing. My passenger (the examiner) really doesn't know what he wants so he's asking me to do this and that. Oh yeah, he can be a jerk too. I'm in command and not my passenger. Once I mentally let the examiner take control, I'm through, washed out. With my imagination running the show, which comes naturally for me, I'm at ease. No more going into the bathroom and crying.

I walked in to Mr. Robinson's office and introduced myself. He's a nice-enough man who's been with the FAA in West Texas forever. I handed him my logbook. (It contained all the flight hours that I've logged both civilian and military.) Since I forgot the aircraft logbooks out in the airplane (ADD kicking in), I excused myself and went to retrieve them. When I walked back into his office, he said, "Marc, when you came in here, I noticed that you're a young man (just turned twenty-one); but when I looked at your logbook, I noticed that you've got a lot of experience."

That's it. I knew that I passed the check ride unless I did something really dumb. The oral and flight test was going to be just a formality. I passed.

Now I felt like I could really make it in the civilian aviation world. I have a flight instructor's certificate. I have some authority.

So I started to instruct a few students and fly pipeline on Monday and half a day on Tuesday. The rest of the time, I flew charters. I made a base pay of $300 a month and $5 per flight hour. Not great, but I was flying and loving it. However, I did miss flying helicopters.

I didn't really want to get into the band thing again, but I did want to get some marijuana. It was a bad habit that I enjoyed. But I had to be very careful. It was a felony to possess any amount of marijuana and if caught I'd go to prison, and my flying career would be over with. That's a heavy price to pay for a little rest and relaxation.

I remembered an old friend that I played in the band with, Gary Barr. We were pretty wild together, so I figured he would be a good source for some weed. I went by his house one night; and sure enough, he was still living with his mother. It was nice seeing him and his mom again. But he had really changed. Not only did he not have any marijuana, he was now one of Jehovah's Witnesses! He began to preach to me about how we're living in the time of the end and so forth. I was trying to get away when he asked me if I would believe it if I saw it in my own copy of the Bible. I actually remembered back to just a few months earlier when I asked my maintenance copilot to show me in the Bible the same stuff.

I said, "Yeah, I'd like to see it."

For the next couple of hours he showed me that and whole lot more. It actually sounded logical but I had a real hard time believing that everything that I was taught as a Presbyterian could be that far off. Hmmm, I wonder if Pam would mail me some marijuana.

"It's been nice seeing you, Gary, and we'll see you later."

CHAPTER 23

Civilian Flying: Pipeline Patrol

O ne of the flying assignments that I enjoyed the most was flying pipeline. Dick had a contract with Mid-America Pipeline to patrol their propane lines once a week. It ran from Hobbs east to San Angelo and then north to just east of Amarillo. Then another shorter line went from Hobbs west to Artesia. It was about a day and a half worth of flying in a Piper Cherokee 140. You wouldn't think that a low-wing aircraft would be well suited for flying pipeline; but actually, it worked quite well. You'd watch your line at your two o'clock position (I flew from the right seat); and then when I needed to take a close look at something, I'd lower the wing into a steep bank and have a nice view of the pipeline, coyote, deer, or whatever else that I'd find interesting. Flying pipeline was also nice because I didn't have to babysit anybody. I was alone with my thoughts. However, the biggest problem I found flying pipeline was falling asleep, especially in the summertime when it was hot and rough. The turbulence made me feel like I was in my mother's arms.

There were also neat things to see, like the time I was flying the pipeline east of Lubbock and came across a flock of ducks flying south for the winter. I slowed the Cherokee down and lowered the flaps so that I was flying just above a stall. (Speed in which the aircraft lacks, the airspeed to maintain flight.) I joined their V formation just off the last duck. That last duck on the right side just stared at me while he continued flying south. Unbeknownst to him, the rest of his formation broke off to the left, but he just kept flying south while looking at me. He then glanced back toward where his fellow aviators should have been, and he actually did a double take and then broke off after them, leaving me laughing.

Or then there was the time while I was flying the line out west of San Angelo, and I flew over a calf that was stuck in the mud. It was struggling to get out of a pond that was almost dried up. The mother cow stood helplessly above its calf. I couldn't help but feel sorry for the calf. I'd like to help, but the terrain was much too rough to attempt a landing; and I was out in the middle of nowhere. About that time, I saw a pickup driving down the dirt road trailing a plume of dust. The truck was going to pass within twenty yards of the pond, but it wasn't visible to the driver because of the vegetation. I quickly wrote a note: "There was a calf stuck in the mud just off to your left." I then made a low pass in front of the pickup and dropped the note that was attached to a small bag of sand and a long colored streamer. It landed just in front of the truck. He saw it! The West Texas rancher slowly got out of his pickup, bent over, picked up the note, and read it. He then slowly turned and went back to his truck, got a rope out, and started to make his way through the brush toward the pond. All the while, I was going back and forth, buzzing the calf. He roped the calf like a true cowboy and after some effort pulled it out of the gooey mess. He never did look up at me nor did he wave thank you. Nope, he gave no indication of appreciation. Oh well, I bet the momma cow appreciated me.

I loved flying pipeline. I could chase antelopes and rescue cows; plus whenever I had to go to the bathroom, which was now quite often, if I didn't have a Sic-Sac, I would land in a field or on a road and take care of business.

On one occasion, I decided that I had to go real bad, and there weren't any Sic-Sacs left. So I decided to land the little Cherokee on a country road. Everything looked good on my high reconnaissance so I set up my approach to land to the west into the wind. Just as I flared the Cherokee about twenty feet above the ground, I saw the telephone wires that crossed the road right in front of me. I didn't have time to go over them so I pushed forward on the elevator causing the nose to go down toward the ground. Then as soon as I pushed forward, I pulled back on the elevator so that the nose came back up and *bam!* the main landing gear wheels hit the road. Power off, I stood on the brakes. (The brakes were on the top part of the rudder pedals.) My sweet little bird and I made it under the wires without a scratch. I got out and took care of business and waved at a lady as she drove around the Cherokee, which was parked half on the road and half in the ditch. Oh, the look on her face. I thought, I really need to get more Sic-Sacs.

What did I do with the full bags? I know it was gross, but I'd pretend that I was a World War I ace, dropping bombs on the enemy. Oil field tanks were my enemy. I couldn't help but laugh at the thought of an oil field worker finding the Sic-Sac and wondering where in the world it came from.

CHAPTER 24

Civilian Flying: New Problem

Teaching people to fly was OK. It was flying, and you got to teach something you love to someone who really wanted that same feeling. However, flying charters was a nice break, but it had its own drawbacks. Since my bladder was messed up from the infection that I had up until recently, I couldn't go very long without having to take a leak; and that could get embarrassing.

For example, one day I was to take a man and his wife to Houston in Dick's Comanche 180. I think they were going to a funeral or something. About forty-five minutes out of Houston, I realized that I'd held it as long as I could. I was fidgeting like a little boy who really, really had to go to the bathroom. There was nothing but trees below us; and since we didn't have DME and GPS hadn't been invented yet, I wasn't quite sure where we were and where the closest airport was. But I knew from the VOR that we were headed straight for Houston International. I couldn't take it anymore!

I turned to the man who was sitting next to me, "Sir, could you have your wife look out the window; I've got to go." He turned and said something to his wife who was sitting behind him. They both were smiling as she turned to look out. I pulled out a Sic-Sac and, while flying with my knees, unfastened the seat belt and pulled down my pants and whew! The relief now turned to embarrassment!

CHAPTER 25

Civilian Flying: Charters

Now that the statute of limitations has expired, I can share the events of another charter. On a Friday afternoon, I flew by myself from Hobbs to Denver's Arapaho airport, (now called Centennial) where my folks picked me up to spend the night. I was to pick up a businesswoman the next morning and fly her back to Hobbs. That night I called my charter to confirm when and where I was to meet her. Strangest thing though, she wanted me to come by where she was staying and pay her a visit; and she was quite persistent! I couldn't understand why though; I didn't know her; we'd never even met. The next day, her strange behavior continued. We met at the airport, and it turned out that she was quite a looker. I must say that I was really distracted. I called the FAA's Flight Service Station and checked the weather and the NOTAMS. NOTAMS stands for "notices to airmen" and contains information about runway closures, radio navigation aids that are out of service, and any other event that would affect the pilot's flight. For our flight, it included an air show in Clovis, New Mexico. We were to pass right over Clovis, but that wasn't going to be a problem. I'd just swing out west of Clovis to avoid the area.

We lifted off Arapaho on Saturday morning; and I figured that in the 180 horsepower single-engine Comanche, we'd make a fuel stop in Raton, New Mexico, in about an hour. All the way to Raton, my passenger told me how much she wanted me, how she found me attractive, and so on . . . My goodness, this was my first (and only) experience with an older woman who knew exactly what she wanted and didn't mind describing her intentions! And quite frankly, I didn't know how to handle it. After leaving Raton, she continued her seduction; and it was working. My head was rushing, and my attention was diverted to her . . . well. What in the world did I think I was going to do five thousand feet above the ground in the cockpit of a small airplane? Didn't matter, I was in heat. We continued southeast toward Clovis. Remembering that they were having an air show, I decided to fly west of Clovis, over Cannon Air Force Base. At about ten miles out, I called Cannon approach control to get traffic advisories and separation from other aircraft.

"Cannon approach, Comanche 9545 Papa . . ."

There was a lot of talking going on, but no response to my call. We continued toward Cannon, indicating 9,500 feet above sea level (five thousand feet above the ground), plenty high enough to be out of their traffic area, even for jets. I called again, but still no answer; and there was still a lot of chatter on the radio. Man, they're busy, I thought. Oh well, I was an ex-military pilot, and I wasn't intimidated or concerned. Anyway, the controller was probably just an enlisted man. As we approached the airbase consisting of acres and acres of concrete, I looked down and saw an awful lot of people, aircraft, and vehicles on the ramp. Huh? I wondered what's going on. Then I saw them. The Air Force Thunderbirds in a diamond formation making a low pass right in front of the crowds. Oh CRAP! We were right in the middle of the air show. I watched with dread as they made another low pass . . . Oh no! Here they come, straight up! They couldn't have been more than a hundred yards away when they screamed past us, in a beautiful, tight diamond formation. I could see every detail of their F-4 jets. Man, that was too close! I don't think they even saw us, except maybe the lead aircraft; but he couldn't do anything about it. Unfortunately, we hadn't dodged the bullet yet. I'd seen this routine before, and they'll all separate somewhere above us into a cloverleaf and then go into a dive in four different directions.

A little too late, Cannon approach called over the radio in a firm voice, "Comanche 4596 Papa, stay out of our area; we're having an air show."

"Roger that, Cannon approach," I replied. I couldn't get that airplane to move fast enough. I remembered when we were taking fire in Vietnam, when we were a sitting duck. Still a sitting duck, but now it was jets coming at us. We had to get out of here! I sacrificed some altitude and began a descent in order to gain airspeed. We slowly flew out of the Cannon Air Force Base traffic area. Dodged the bullet again.

After the dread of a possible midair mishap passed, then came the dread of possible FAA action. Did they know who it was that flew through the middle of their air show? I never heard from anybody, and I sure wasn't going to confess like Captain Petzold who lost his prisoner.

I did influence one positive outcome from that day. Now whenever there's a military air show, they post a spotter outside the control tower that looks for aircraft straying into their airspace, like the Comanche being flown by one distracted pilot.

During those last few minutes before our landing in Hobbs, I reflected on the flight, the seduction, the near-midair mishap, and my lack of professionalism. Not just as a professional pilot but as an employee and a Presbyterian too.

"I've got to clean up my act. I can't continue to go around like I'm in heat looking for anything that wore a skirt," I said, half to myself and half to God, if there is one listening.

I guess I'd been flying for Dick for about two months when he scheduled me to take two oilmen from Hobbs to Meacham Field in Fort Worth, Texas. This was the same airport where the Acme School of Aeronautics and Linda Sue were located. My passengers were to conduct business for a couple of hours, and then I was to fly them back to Hobbs. While waiting for my passengers, I had lunch with Linda Sue. After lunch, I couldn't think of anything to say, so I asked her, "Why don't you come back to Hobbs with me?" (Who in their right mind would believe a line like that?)

Linda Sue asked me, as if she was calling my bluff, "Are you serious?"

Still refusing to believe that she could possibly believe that I was serious, I replied, "Sure."

After saying OK, she was out the door and on her way home to pack. OH MY! I thought, now what do I do? Maybe my passengers will get here before she does. "Too bad, had to go; passengers were waiting." Yeah, that would be my response. That is if I ever saw her again. No such luck. She was back in a flash. She must have had everything already packed and stashed in her little VW bug. Linda Sue walked in to her boss's office and just quit her job! Oh boy, now I really was committed. We sat in the small terminal seating area and chitchatted for about an hour.

When my passengers showed up, I pulled the two men aside and asked, "I've got a problem; do you mind if we take someone back with us since we have an extra seat?" For some reason, they thought that this was hilarious. "Yeah, sure, no problem" was their response.

During the flight back to Hobbs, I would glance at Linda Sue and offer her a weak smile, while thinking, where is this going? I had never been in this position before.

After we landed, I took Linda Sue and her belongings over to my brother to stay. Jeff and his wife Karen were very

Linda Sue on the Comanche

accommodating. I think they were finally ready for me to get married. I got the marriage certificate; and Jeff and Karen arranged for a Baptist minister to come over to the house, and we got married. Wow! What happened? Never again would I have girlfriends everywhere I went. No more multiple fiancés. I finally met my match, or rather I met my mate. OK, I think I'm ready to settle down.

We were married on a Monday afternoon, had a wedding supper with Jeff and Karen at Furrs Cafeteria, and then moved into an apartment that night. The next morning at 7:00 a.m., I was up flying pipeline. So much for a honeymoon. We didn't have much, but we were happy.

Shortly after the wedding

CHAPTER 26

The Return of the Dreaded Dread

Dick wanted me to get my multiengine rating so that I could instruct and fly charters in his Twin Comanche. The Twin Comanche is a light multiengine airplane with either four or six seats. Since Dick was the only other instructor at Marshall Aviation, by default, he was my instructor. I trusted Dick. He was old enough to be my dad and had been flying since he was a kid. His dad, Tex Marshall, was an old-time mail pilot who used to keep anyone who would listen mesmerized with his stories. When I didn't have a student, charter, or a pipeline to fly, Dick and I would fly in the twin, which meant my training was taking the slow-boat route.

After about ten hours of dual, Dick said, "Marc, as an instructor, you're going to need to know how to get out of a single-engine stall."

Now I heard about the terrible reputation that the Twin Comanche had for getting into a flat spin and that those poor pilots who slipped up and went flat were doomed because there's no way to recover from it. But I really didn't put two and two together to come up with the fact that this was the maneuver that caused their demise.

It was a nice day in September when we climbed into the Twin Comanche for what was to be the lesson on how to recover from a single-engine stall. We took off and headed northwest out of Hobbs Lea County Airport, which was located five miles west of town. "Take it up to 9,500 feet," Dick requested. It didn't take us long to reach what was about five thousand feet above the ground. I was in the left seat, and Dick was in the right. We went over all the procedures on the ground, but he repeated them again in a matter-of-fact way.

"We're going to pull the power off the right engine. Try to hold her straight, but you won't be able to. It will go over on its back into a spin, and you won't be able to stop it. We'll recover by pulling the power off the good engine and then make a normal power-off spin recovery." (That was to relax the rearward pressure on the elevator as you apply the full left rudder, opposite the direction of the spin, and then smoothly raise the nose.)

"OK, Marc, you have the controls, and I've got the quadrant (engine power controls)," Dick instructed.

He pulled the power back to idle on the right engine but didn't feather the prop. That meant that the propeller was wind milling rather than streamlining into the wind, which would have produced less drag. I raised the nose slightly and started to slow the aircraft down while at the same time pressing hard on the left rudder to keep it in trim.

Sure enough, I couldn't keep it straight. As if it had a mind of its own, she started a hard roll to the right and on its back. Dick said, "OK, I've got the controls." Immediately my hands and feet left the controls. I raised both hands as if to say "Whoa"; so Dick could see that I was clearly off the controls, although he didn't look. The aircraft pitched almost straight down and began a very tight spin. Dick pulled the power back off the left engine; and as he pressed hard on the left rudder, he started to raise the aircraft's nose. The spin went flat.

Did we really go flat? I asked myself. Airspeed sixty knots, a moderately tight spin with a slight nose-down attitude. Yep, we went flat, and that wasn't good! Our rate of descent, or how fast we were falling out of the sky, was 1,500 feet per minute. No, wait, it was two thousand feet . . . Didn't matter, we were falling out of the sky; and in about two minutes, we'd be dead. Instantly, my thoughts went to those who had died before us in the Twin Comanche. This wasn't a feeling of bonding, as if we were going through this together or that we were going to have the same fate. Rather, what did they do to try to get out of the spin, and why didn't it work; or did they just freeze, cry, or pray?

I looked over at Dick. He was as white as a sheet and uttering profanities. *Goddamn* seemed to be his favorite. He had just finished again trying the standard power-off spin-recovery method that he had explained to me just seconds earlier. Now he added full power to both engines and then pushed the yoke or the elevators full forward. This was an attempt to fly out of the spin . . . and nothing happened.

The last thing I wanted Dick to do was freeze or get religious on me and try to get right with God, whom he was actively asking to damn the aircraft. I now asked Dick in a clear, louder-than-normal voice, but with no hint of panic, "Dick, didn't you say to pull the power off the good engine and recover with the power off?"

"Goddamn, nothing is working; nothing is working . . . goddamn!"

Now he pulled the power off the left engine and added full power to the right engine, opposite to the rotation of the aircraft. Good move, I thought, but it didn't work. Dick was trying everything he could think of. All the years of experience, knowledge of aerodynamics, and luck weren't working; nothing was working. The elevators, ailerons, rudders, and all the controls were dead.

The spin didn't increase or decrease in intensity. I looked out my side window and could actually see the headlines from the Hobbs newspaper: "Two Hobbs Men Crash North of Town." (We were actually west of town, but newspaper reporters can never get aircraft accidents right.) Surprisingly, I wasn't on the verge of panic, nor was I emotional about my impending death. I thought of all the close calls I had in Vietnam where I could have just as easily died as lived. How about that, I lived through it all just to die in a civilian accident. I couldn't restrain a brief chuckle.

I now thought to myself, We need to get our center of gravity farther forward, which would cause the nose to pitch down, perhaps just enough to pick up some airspeed and fly out of the spin. So I unfastened my seatbelt and put my arms forward on top of the instrument panel and climbed as far forward as possible. While I was doing this, Dick reached for the elevator trim tab, located on the ceiling between us, and rolled it to the full forward position. This would give the elevator a little more forward motion, allowing the nose to pitch down just a little more. Whatever we did, it worked! We broke out of spin!

There was silence except for the engines that were pulsating because they were horribly out of sink. We didn't care or try to harmonize them. We immediately turned toward Hobbs and started the five-minute flight back. Neither one of us said a word; nor did we care that the right engine was surging from idle to red line then back, again and again.

Dick called the tower, "Hobbs tower, niner five four five papa five miles northwest landing."

"Roger, four five papa, make a straight into runway twelve, cleared to land." I must say the tower operator's voice sounded good.

After we touched down, the tower cleared us to taxi to Marshall Aviation. I thought to myself that if they only knew what just took place . . . We pulled up in front of the hangar and shut the engines down. Since there was only one door up front and it was on the right side, Dick climbed out first and I followed him. Dick went straight into his office. I lingered getting out of the aircraft and slowly climbed down off the wing, as if savoring the fact that we didn't die. As my feet touched the ground, I noticed a large pool of fuel under the right engine. I bent down to see where it was coming from. It had been pouring out from the bottom of the right engine cowling. It turned out that we were spinning so hard that we broke the fuel injector off the right engine! Not only should we have died from that flat spin, hell, we should have been a fireworks show too.

After everything that I went through in Vietnam, all those encounters where we crossed back and forth over that thin line that separates a close call from a statistic, I almost died as a civilian. I still loved to fly but not in multiengine aircraft.

This close call really affected me. Did God pull us out of the flat spin? Does he go around making up for my poor decisions and mistakes? Was I a better person than those who died in Vietnam or in the Twin Comanche before me, so that God saved me and not them? No, I don't think so. If God did that, with my moral track record, he would have struck me down a long time ago. I did know this. If I was killed today and went to face my maker, I'd be in bad shape, even for Presbyterian standards. I think I'll give Gary a call.

CHAPTER 27

Moving On

I continued to work for Dick until Linda Sue became pregnant with Jason, our first of two children. Since Linda Sue wanted and needed to be near her mother, we moved to Fort Worth. Flying jobs were hard to come by; and pilots were a dime a dozen, seeing that the Vietnam War was winding down and the airlines were laying off their pilots. So I took a job as an aviation insurance underwriter. I was assigned an eight-state region where I made safety inspections and sold insurance to qualified flight schools, fixed base operators (FBOs), maintenance shops, and charter operators. I was furnished a new Cessna 182 RG and a credit card. I must say that this was quite enjoyable. I flew from North Dakota down through the central states, including Colorado and New Mexico, landing at every airport that I could find. Although the flying was enjoyable, it was not without perils.

While flying IFR (in the clouds) from Fort Worth to Houston Intercontinental Airport (HAI), I lost my communication radios.

I could no longer hear Houston Center, and I was about to be handed off to Houston Approach Control. According to the Federal Aviation Regulations, I was to continue on my filed flight plan route to HIA and then make an instrument approach. This would hold up all the corporate and airline aircraft wanting to land or take off. I was about to cause a tremendous snarl in air traffic that would reverberate across the country. About thirty miles outside of Houston, I flew into a break in the clouds and could see the ground. Before I could fly back into the clouds, I pulled the power back, lowered the landing gear and flaps, and dove the aircraft toward the ground. At about five hundred feet above the ground, I leveled the plane; I was below the overcast. From there I "scud run" to Tom Ball, a small airport just outside of Houston, and landed. Houston Approach Control was very appreciative that I got out of their airspace. The problem? A short in the speaker system.

And then there were other times like when I was descending out of altitude to land at Lamar, Colorado. Since it was a beautiful, calm day, I pushed the airspeed high up into the yellow. Flying in the yellow arch of the airspeed indicator was allowed only if the air was smooth. The Cessna 182 RG, one of the best single engine retractable gear aircraft ever made, was hauling ass. Then from my top left side came a B-1 bomber. He was in a descending right turn, also hauling ass, and flew right in front of me, perhaps one or two blocks away. As fast as I could say "OH MY!" I hit his wake. Any other aircraft might have come apart, but not this one. I ricocheted off the ceiling, and everything in the plane was flying everywhere. I thought for sure that we were coming apart in midair, especially when I heard a loud rushing noise. The left door popped open. With memories of the midair collision that I witnessed at Marble Mountain on my mind, I landed safely in Lamar.

But for the most part, those fifteen years of flying for the insurance company were uneventful and most enjoyable. I saw some of the most beautiful spots on this planet. I guess, on my list of favorites was the Mount Zirkel, which is just northeast of Steamboat Springs, Colorado. The natural lakes that pepper the twelve-thousand-foot mountain take your breath away. Then there's the unique beauty of the Big Bend area of Texas, Alpine, and Marfa. I always loved the desert moutains. Those were good years and the joy of flight far outweighed the rare moments of terror.

Linda Sue and I lived in Texas for almost twenty-three years. We raised two wonderful children there, and although Fort Worth was good to us, I was ready for a change. Our son, Jason, married a beautiful girl from Hawaii and moved to Decatur, Texas, and shortly thereafter, our little girl, Melissa, married a nice young man and moved to Arlington, Texas. Finally, we were free.

Linda Sue and I decided to move to the mountains of Utah, where I took a job as a director in the Utah Valley State College's (UVSC) Aviation Science Program. While there, I put together a corporate partnership with Diamond Aircraft,

Me in a Katana over Provo
(Photo courtesy of the Provo Daily Herald)

a Canadian aircraft manufacturer. They furnished us a Diamond Katana (DA-20C) that I demonstrated to flight schools across the United States. It was an outstanding aircraft that was a true joy to fly. But flying cross-country was taking its toll on my health, especially my bladder. Trying to fly a small stick-controlled airplane (like the cyclic in the helicopter) and peeing into a Sic-Sac while flying with your knees can be quite a challenge.

After a couple of years, I left UVSC to become the executive director of a national flight school association; and at the same time, I started flight instructing at a local helicopter flight school. I must say the Robinson R22 was a handful and was much more difficult to fly than Blivit; but it felt good to pull up to a three-foot hover once again.

CHAPTER 28

Crash and Burn

> Shortly after a traumatic event, such as combat . . . or a
> serious accident, during which a person has experienced
> intense fear, most people will experience anxiety and may
> have recurrent intrusive thoughts about the event. In some
> people, these persist long after and are now considered to
> constitute post-traumatic stress disorder (PTSD).

> – I. P. Christensen

After my tour of duty in Vietnam, I chose to put all those experiences, good and bad, in a little box in the back of my mind, never to be seriously considered again other than for elaborating to a new student pilot what it is like to have a midair collision. But the past wasn't through with me.

The opening of the box began in 1997 when I went to my urologist because of the worsening side effects of my bad bladder.

During the routine finger examination that all men love, he discovered a lump on my prostate. He wasn't too concerned since my PSA count was 2.2, which was normal for a man my age. So he suggested we try antibiotics for six weeks, but the lump was still there. Now more concerned, he recommended a biopsy. I reluctantly agreed. It came back positive.

This knocked me for a loop. I was OK until I went into our bedroom and told Linda Sue that the doctor just called and said I had cancer. I was actually quite surprised when I started crying; then she started crying. I don't think I've cried since the day that Browne busted me on my private pilot check ride. I must say that this whole cancer experience drew Linda Sue and me ever closer together. She stood behind me every step of what I was about to face.

I contacted the VA (veteran's administration) after reading a report about Agent Orange causing prostate cancer. My experience with the VA was much different than my last dealing with them in 1971 when I applied for disability for my bad bladder. They treated me like I was trying to con the poor innocent government out of its last dollar. This time they were very kind and considerate. My VA urologist said, "Forty-six-year-old men don't get prostate cancer." So my request for disability was rubber-stamped "Approved." The VA attributed my cancer to Agent Orange, which was routinely used in the mountains just west of Quang Tri. Since my bladder was already damaged by the infection, I couldn't risk losing what bladder control I had left with chemo or radiation. So I tried alternative treatments, herbs, and spices. This seemed to work for about a year. But after further tests by the VA, it became evident that my prostate was going to have to be removed.

There was one positive thing that came out of the many tests and scopings that I had to endure. During a bladder biopsy (the

VA wanted to make sure that the cancer didn't go up into my bladder), they found that my bladder was actually damaged from the infection. I felt vindicated! If they had performed a bladder biopsy twenty-five years ago, they would have believed me and awarded me the disability that I deserved. Oh well.

I decided to go ahead and get it over with and had my prostate removed. The surgery and care I received was excellent. The prostatectomy was none too soon. The cancer was starting to spread, but the surgeons thought that they got it all. Ha, I dodged the bullet again. Everybody puts so much weight on the PSA test. If I had waited until it was elevated to have the operation, the cancer would have killed me. It was only 2.5 when the prostate was removed. The cancer was on the outside of my prostate.

It was right after my operation that I slipped into a deep depression and a mental fog. Linda Sue assured me that this was not unusual after such a serious operation. But the depression and fog didn't go away. My nerves were now always on edge. I was irritable and began to experience anxiety attacks. In the mornings, I would wake up with a terrible stress headache. And since I gave up the heavy drinking a long time ago, I couldn't blame it on the booze. I also developed an OCD (obsessive-compulsive disorder) that fueled my depression. Any little thing would trigger a negative memory of a mistake that I'd made, real or imagined. Believe me, over the last forty years, I'd made a lot of mistakes, and I think every single one of them came back to haunt me. The second guessing and the unnecessary remorse were driving me crazy. Each thought would generate a silent or audible "Damn!" or "Shit!" That was embarrassing. Oh yes, then there was the one song that kept going through my head, and I couldn't get rid of it. "La la la la la Means I Love You," by The Delfonics. That song played every day on the Armed Forces Radio in Vietnam. Yeah, we listened to the radio while flying missions. I was actually starting to wonder if I was going crazy.

My behavior was starting to have a serious effect on our marriage. Linda Sue asked me to go get professional help, but I'd reply that I was OK. Anyway, if I did, the FAA would take away my medical; and I wouldn't be able to fly anymore. My mind was made up. Flying has been part of my entire life, and I wasn't going to give it up.

One night, Linda Sue showed me an article in the *Awake!* magazine (published by the Watchtower Bible and Tract Society). It had to do with mental illness and the fourteen symptoms that indicate that you may have a problem. She said that I displayed eleven of the symptoms. I agreed that I had ten of the fourteen symptoms, but I argued with her about the eleventh, contentiousness. I still didn't seek help.

A couple of months later, after suffering from a bad sinus infection for over a week, I decided to go get some antibiotics at the VA clinic in Orem, Utah. While I was being examined, the nurse started to ask me some questions about how I felt emotionally and about my tour of duty in Vietnam. I answered all of her questions as honestly as I could.

I don't know what I said to scare her, but she finally paused and said, "Marc, you need help; let me take you over to Dr. Lynda Baum. I think she can help you."

Normally, it would take you three months to get in to see a VA mental health care provider, but the nurse took me by the hand and walked me over to Dr. Baum's office. The nurse introduced me and said, "Mr. Williams needs your help." Dr. Baum asked me to sit down. She kindly started to ask me questions. I guess I was in the mood to talk because I rambled on and on for almost an hour.

She finally stopped me and said, "Marc, I think you have post-traumatic stress disorder (PTSD). I'd like to put you on some medication and enroll you in therapy, both private and group. We can help you, Marc."

I replied that I appreciated everything that she was trying to do for me. But if I went down that road, I wouldn't be able to fly anymore.

She said she understood but asked me to think about it and to give her a call if I changed my mind.

I agreed – to think about it, that is.

PTSD? Why me? I didn't ask for this, and I sure didn't choose this course. How could I have PTSD? I always considered that the grunts in Vietnam had it a lot worse than I did.

Dr. Baum didn't wait for me to change my mind. Her receptionist called the next day and said that she had set up an appointment for me that following Tuesday. Man, she really thinks I need help, I thought.

OK, I resigned to the fact that I was sick and decided to let her and the VA give me the help that everyone seemed to think I needed, especially Linda Sue. Yeah, I guess I realized it too.

Dr. Baum put me on Zoloft and scheduled me to see her every month. She highly recommended that I should attend group therapy.

I really didn't want to go to group therapy. I imagined a room full of winos complaining about the war and the VA. Instead, I was warmly welcomed by the VA counselor, Dennis Stevens, a fellow Vietnam veteran, and a dozen men about my age. Some couldn't work, and others were blue-collar workers and businessmen. What really surprised me was that they all thought I was their hero. It turned out that almost all of them were pulled out of a nasty situation in Vietnam by some kids in a Huey. Since they couldn't thank whoever it was that saved them, they decided that I would be their surrogate hero. I've never experienced such appreciation before and was quite taken aback. It was actually a brotherhood of men who understood what I was going through.

It was on the second night of group therapy that I experienced a breakthrough. An air force veteran named Bob, who was assigned to an army unit in Vietnam, commented that he was having nightmares again but still couldn't remember them.

I interrupted him with a time-out signal and asked, "Bob, what do you mean you couldn't remember them? How can they be nightmares if you can't remember them?"

He said, "It's not unusual for a person not to be able to remember their nightmares. I know that I've had one when I wake up depressed and with a headache."

"That's exactly how I feel!" I said.

I was just now starting to understand what was happening to me.

It was a day or two later that I woke up with another stress headache. Instead of routinely taking the three Tylenols with my coffee, I sat down by myself and started to think. What did I dream last night that caused such a headache? I found a memory string and started to pull it in, and then there it was, my nightmare. Although this confirmed that I have been having nightmares, I regretted searching for it. I dreamed that I actually mutilated a man with a baseball bat. It took me several days to get over it. From then on, when I woke up with the headache, I just took the Tylenol.

It was my ninth day on Zoloft when the clouds of depression and mental fog started to part. I actually started to feel good, very good. It was so profound that I remembered where I was and what I was doing. I started to smile and laugh. My marriage took a rapid turn for the better. My friends didn't seem so standoffish anymore. Although I could no longer fly, the good feeling, that I was experiencing made up for it.

After almost a year of personal therapy, group help, and Zoloft, I started the process of learning how to cope with the PTSD without the drugs. With Dr. Baum's help, I learned what to do in order to stay in control of my feelings and what to do when the PTSD symptoms came back. The nightmares finally went away as well as the anxiety attacks, and even those damn OCDs.

It's interesting that Dr. Baum recommended for my therapy that I put my thoughts, memories, and feelings down in writing. So I started to write, write, and write some more. The bottled-up feelings were released, and I cried. I cried for Captain Gene Peterson, I cried for my fellow soldiers on both sides, and I cried for me. A nineteen-year-old boy had no business seeing what I'd seen, experiencing what I experienced, and being put under the pressure to make the decisions that I had to make. As if that nineteen-year-old aircraft commander in Vietnam was someone else, I learned to love him and forgive him. He became my friend.

CHAPTER 29

The End of the Search

Now that I had my head screwed on straight, on which Dr. Baum and the FAA agreed, I got my second-class flight physical back.

I can fly again!

Now at fifty-seven, I can say that the cancer is gone; and I am back doing what I find so satisfying, flying. Flying is like a drug. After I land, I feel so relaxed and calm. My fellow pilots know what I'm talking about. But what I really wanted to do was fly EMS. The idea of helping people who were experiencing a crisis and, at the same time, fly helicopters the way I used to fly them in Vietnam was very appealing to me.

So I started to look into the two EMS operators in the Salt Lake City area. But Linda Sue wanted to move closer to our daughter, Melissa; her husband, Kit; and our two grandchildren, Caleb and Sissy. Yeah, I did too. They reside in the little town of Ashland, Kansas, which is about an hour south of Dodge City.

So when I heard that an EMS company was going to open up a new base in Dodge City, I jumped all over it. We packed up our belongings, sold the house, and moved to Dodge City, home of Wyatt Earp, Matt Dillon, Ms. Kitty, and a very large number of cows. So here I am, back in Kansas, not far from where it all began.

My goose bumps are gone now.

"Life Team 21, this is the LZ commander, we've got an LZ set up in the patient's backyard. There's a large tree to the south, smaller trees to the west, wires to the east; and the farmhouse is to the north. I'm afraid it's going to be a little tight. Oh yeah, the ground slopes toward a pond to the south."

Although we didn't see the fire trucks and ambulances yet, all three of us were now forming a mental picture of the LZ. Katie responded to the report by repeating the descriptions.

The GPS now indicated that we were a little over a minute out, so I called dispatch, "Life Team 21's on a one-minute final."

"Roger, one-minute final," dispatch responded.

As we approached the scene from the southwest, I could now see the emergency equipment with their lights flashing. But where's the LZ? I wondered. OK, there it is. It's just as they described.

"Man, those guys are good," I said out loud.

Paul and Katie didn't respond. After all, they've been working with sheriffs' departments and fire and EMS crews for years; and they already knew that everybody had their job to do and that they were all professionals. Yeah, I was impressed with these guys.

Now the helicopter was sterile; there was no communication except what was necessary for the operation of the helicopter.

As I made a descending half circle around the LZ, I described the LZ to my crew, to make sure that I didn't miss something. Paul and Katie confirmed that that's what they saw.

"OK, we're going to approach from the southeast; then once clear of the wires, I'll be bringing my tail to the left."

Katie responded, "OK, we'll clear your tail."

As I lined up on final approach to the LZ, I glanced at the radar altimeter; and it read 360 feet above the ground. My eyes started dancing from obstacle to obstacle, then to my airspeed for the last time, and then to my vertical speed indicator to make sure we were not about to enter "settling with power."

We were at two hundred feet now, and I could see the fireman who was marking the LZ. I adjusted my glide path so that I was looking at him through my chin bubble. Now it would be like sliding down a string to a point at the feet of the fireman.

So far so good, I thought. I was one with the helicopter. Once again, it felt as if I had strapped this million-dollar machine to my back. Just like in Vietnam. Just like landing *Blivit* in an LZ that's carved out of the jungle on the side a mountain or landing on the back of a hospital ship. I felt like I was doing it all over again, and I loved it.

"You're clear of the wires," Paul called out.

Then, as if waiting her turn, Katie called out, "Your tail's clear left."

"OK, thanks . . . is this close enough to the ambulance?" I asked as we started to descend straight down from a one-hundred-foot hover.

"Yeah, this is fine," Paul responded.

The fireman was now twenty feet off my nose, walking away from the LZ with his back to me so I wouldn't blind him with the dust. After leveling off at a five-foot hover, I slowly lowered the collective until the left skid touched. Now just a little more, and then the right skid touched. I slowly lowered the collective until it was fully down. We're OK, no rocks or other obstacles in the way, and the surface was solid.

"OK, we're down," I called out over the intercom.

That was the signal for Paul to roll into action. He jumped out of the left side of the helicopter and started to half run and half walk toward the waiting entourage of emergency personnel. I glanced over at the friends and relatives of the poor man who was the focus of our mission of mercy, and then at the emergency personnel. At that moment, they were all giving my crew and me the center stage. As I took another deep breath, a swelling of appreciation and relief enveloped me.

I smiled at the thought that I'm OK. Yeah, I'm going to be just fine. No relapses, no PTSD, no OCDs. That's all behind me now. I've dealt with it and won. Yes! I still love to fly, and I'm still damn good.

Paul, Katie, and two of the firemen were now approaching the helicopter with the stretcher. They quickly loaded the man, who looked like he was about my age, into the helicopter. The firemen retreated back to their fire truck while Paul and Katie climbed into their seats and plugged in their helmets.

"OK, we're ready, let's go to KU Med Center," Katie said. (That's just south of downtown Kansas City.)

Taking just a second before pulling pitch, I looked at everyone that was a part of our patient's life and those attempting to extend it, standing there with their eyes fixed on us. I realized that I'd found something that makes me truly happy; helping others who need help spiritually and physically with whatever experiences, talents or gifts, like ADD and emotional baggage, that I may have.

"Coming up," I called out over the intercom as I pulled pitch, straight up for one hundred feet until the huge cottonwood tree on my left was cleared; and then we were off to Kansas City.

Yeah . . . for the love of flight.